CLASSIC HOLES *of* GOLF

CLASSIC HOLES of GOLF

A Grand Tour of the World's Most Challenging, Historic, and Beautiful Golf Holes

Robert Green and Brian Morgan

PRENTICE HALL PRESS

New York · London · Toronto · Sydney · Tokyo

PRENTICE HALL PRESS

Gulf+Western Building
One Gulf+Western Plaza
New York, New York 10023

Simultaneously published in Great Britain
by William Collins Sons & Co. Ltd

PRENTICE HALL PRESS and colophon
are registered trademarks of
Simon & Schuster, Inc.

Library of Congress Cataloging in Publication Data

Green, Robert, 1953 –
Glassic holes of golf/Robert Green and Brian Morgan
p   cm
Includes index
ISBN: 0-13-138009-5: $29.95
1. Golf Courses   I. Morgan, Brian, 1946 –   II. Title
GV975.G74 1989   89–30660
796.352′06′8–dc19   CIP

Set in Novarese Book by Bookworm Typesetting, Manchester
Color Origination by Bright Arts (Hong Kong) Ltd
Printed and bound in Great Britain by William Collins
Sons & Co. Ltd, Glasgow

10 9 8 7 6 5 4 3 2 1

First Prentice Hall Press Editon

Contents

Introduction

If one rather stretches the point, it may be that man's fascination with the beauty and challenge of the game of golf can be traced back to the very existence of mankind. To quote one great writer, Alistair Cooke, on the work of another knowledgeable commentator and meticulous researcher:

'Sir Guy Campbell's classic account of the formation of the links beginning with Genesis and moving step by step to the thrilling arrival of "tilth" on the fingers of coastal land suggests that such notable features of our planet as dinosaurs, the prairies, the Himalayas, the seagull, the female of the species herself, were accidental by-products of the Almighty's preoccupation with the creation of the Old Course at St Andrews.'

From the formation of the oldest championship golf course in the world on the east coast of Scotland we have 'progressed' to the construction of one of the newest: Oak Tree in Oklahoma, site of the 1988 US PGA Championship, where the owner, Joe Walser, said of the course architect, Pete Dye: 'I gave him an unlimited budget and he exceeded it.'

On seeing the Old Course for the first time, Sam Snead, who won the 1946 Open Championship there ('British Open' to American readers, of which more later) remarked that it looked 'so raggedy and beat up I was surprised to see what looked like fairway among the weeds. Down home we wouldn't plant cow beets on land like that.' Pete Dye, in considering how penal his creation could be made for the PGA Championship, noted: 'If they make the rough too tough or the greens too slick, a lot of guys aren't going to finish out there at all.' From an inadequate vegetable pasture to a war zone. The difference? One was built by the Almighty, the other at an almighty cost. For the former there was no need for a budget; for the latter a lot of money was evidently not enough.

But it isn't easy to make cheap shots about a course as meritorious as Oak Tree. It was too expensive to build, for a start, and many holes on it extract shots as painfully as teeth. And yet it is almost ironic that the 1984 Open Championship at St Andrews was won with a total which was 12 shots below par. The winning score at the 1988 PGA was also 12 under par. *Plus ça change, plus c'est la même chose. . . .*

St Andrews and Oak Tree are at different ends of the golfing spectrum, separated not merely by some 6000 miles but by at least four centuries in age (and maybe double that), by vastly different architectural and financial origins, and by the different types of golf they offer. But both the 17th hole at St Andrews and the 4th hole at Oak Tree, both of which are featured here, deserve to be included in a book that tries to depict something of the flavour of this great game. They are very different from each other but they are both great holes.

The choice of holes herein is intended to reflect the wide international spread of golf and its varied styles of course design and terrain: links, heathland and parkland courses (the former generally being built on a sandy subsoil while the latter run over heavier arable land), mountain courses, exotic locations, courses constructed at great expense from the wilderness, and the simply spectacular.

There are 32 holes from the United States, which, not surprisingly, can justifiably claim to have more great courses in its possession than any other country. There are 22 from the British Isles, where the game began, and for this purpose the British Isles includes the Irish Republic. There are 18 holes from elsewhere around the world: from the continent of Europe, Canada, the Caribbean, Africa, Asia, Australasia and South America. The hope of Brian Morgan and myself is that this book will give you a feeling for each hole and that, even if you have never played it and are never likely to, the compelling, alluring attraction of the game, as made manifest by these photographs, will have been captured by the camera – even if in some cases what the lens has brought into focus is a shot so scary that it is more successfully, if not satisfyingly, attempted with a camera than with a golf club.

Although every picture tells a story, it cannot always tell the whole story. To do that would largely have restricted the book to photos of par-3 holes, but the game is too big to be confined to 250 yards or less every time. In fact, there are 'only' 23 par-3s in the book, with the other 49 holes consisting of 40 par-4s and 9 par-5s. Of the 72 pictures, 43 are taken from in front of the green, 29 from behind it – albeit that precise distinction is blurred occasionally by a few shots having been taken from unusual angles where nobody but a young Seve Ballesteros would have expected to be – but the configuration and topography of many holes means that it is impossible for each of the par-4s and par-5s to be portrayed in all their glory. For that reason, an illustration of each hole, drawn by David Scutt, gives an indication of how it plays and where its significant hazards and landmarks are situated. Our intention is that this guide will complement the photograph and enhance your appreciation of the design of our 72 selections, though only the photograph can show the visual appeal of the hole. If the picture makes you want to play it, we have succeeded in our choice.

That is far from saying that our choice will be greeted with unanimous approval. This book is published in the sure knowledge that absolutely everybody who reads it will feel justified in pointing out at least one serious omission, either by suggesting that we have excluded a course which should have been in or by complaining that while we have the right course we have selected the wrong hole. Both possibilities (make that certainties) can only be countered by acknowledging that this is inevitably and essentially a subjective topic, and by asserting that each choice is defendable. Apart from the fact that each hole has to be photogenic in order to be compatible with the aims of the book, they each have further reasons for being within these pages.

First, there are examples of classic holes. I say 'first' partly because the first course to be featured in this book is Augusta National in Georgia, the home of the Masters Tournament. Most holes at Augusta look nearly as good on paper as they do in reality, and many would have done justice to this book. The 13th is just one of many great holes on Augusta's magnificent and malevolent back nine, probably the most well-known stretch of golfing ground in the world given its annual exposure via our television screens each April when the Masters invariably comes to a thrilling conclusion. And the 13th is a hole of classic design, perhaps the perfect exemplification of a short par-5.

If that may be one of the most photographed holes in the world, the most feared may be the 17th at St Andrews: the 'Road Hole'. It, too, is a classic. Arguably no par-4 anywhere else is as terrifying as this one, though Jack Nicklaus has almost reproduced it in reverse on the New Course at Grand Cypress in Florida, a layout unashamedly modelled on the Old Course at St Andrews (the South Course at Grand Cypress is included here), and the hole has been copied less obviously and less ostentatiously at other places down the ages. It has had a seminal influence on course design throughout the world.

Nicklaus, in addition to being probably the greatest professional golfer in history, is one of the foremost golf course architects of the modern era. America's first eminent course architect, Charles Blair Macdonald, built the National Golf Links of America (see page 78) following extensive and detailed visits to golf courses in Europe, especially to the links of England and Scotland. During his time in Britain, Macdonald discovered that the Road Hole was considered by the experts to be Britain's best 'three-shot' hole. That is still the way it plays for most people today, as a par-5, and even that judgment might do the hole less than justice. Two recent incidents, from the 1988 Dunhill Nations Cup, could appropriately be added to the catalogue of catastrophes referred to on page 128. Mark Mouland of Wales didn't play the 17th as a three-shotter in his match against David Graham of Australia. He needed seven blows merely to travel the few feet to the green from the hideous Road Bunker. Then, in the final, Australia effectively turned victory into defeat when Rodger Davis sliced his tee shot out-of-bounds and ceded the initiative, and shortly afterwards the lead and the match, to Des Smyth of Ireland. Davis's third shot was his second drive. No hole in golf has withstood the passage of time, the vast improvements in equipment and the generally higher standard of play better than the Road Hole.

So from Augusta we have a classic, nominal three-shotter where the green can comfortably be reached in two, and from St Andrews a classic, nominal two-shotter where even the best players in the game frequently try to make par by getting on in three with a chip and then sinking a putt. A classic short hole is the 7th at Pebble Beach, in California, a 107-yard, downhill par-3. But although Carl Lewis could cover the distance in less than 10 seconds, without the wind or anything else to assist him, it can take a handicap golfer anything from a wood to a wedge to reach the target. Short holes do not have to be long to be tough, and the backdrop to this hole (see page 92) emphasizes that it is characterized by its presence on one of the most magnificent coastlines known to man – that of the Pacific Ocean.

The three aforementioned holes are renowned throughout the world, as are the courses which they grace. As I indicated earlier, Augusta National could have been equally well represented by many other holes – the 12th, 15th or 16th, for example. At St Andrews it could have been the 1st, the 11th or the 14th. Pebble Beach's cause would have been served with just as much distinction by the 8th, the 17th or the 18th. The same sort of thing is true with regard to the second set of examples: the historic holes. Certainly, the selections from the three courses already discussed have been the scenes of events destined to be forever remembered in golfing lore, but at the likes of Cherry Hills, Merion and Royal Troon one hole stands out above the others, marvellous courses though they, too, are in their entireties.

At Cherry Hills it had to be the opener, the hole where Arnold Palmer proved to himself that he could win the 1960 US Open. It is rare that, even with a generous portion of licence, one can claim that the outcome of a major championship was settled on the first hole of the final round, but that is what may have occurred on that summer day in Denver.

At Merion, in Philadelphia, a strong case could be argued for the 18th, where Ben Hogan hit the most famous 1-iron in history to the heart of the green in order to save his par and force a playoff for the 1950 US Open, which he went on to win just over 16 months after a near-fatal car crash had left his legs aching and weary. That was a dramatic day, but one that has to give best to the events which unfolded on the 11th green on the afternoon of 27 September 1930. That was when Bobby Jones clinched the Grand Slam, the most momentous accomplishment in the annals of the sport. And besides that, the 11th is an outstanding, shortish par-4.

The 8th at Troon, on Scotland's Ayrshire coast, is, like the 7th at Pebble Beach, a short short hole, long on tradition if not on distance. Two of its most oft-recounted tales are repeated on page 126.

The choice of holes at some of the other courses was harder to make. All that was certain was that the courses had to be in here. The wonderful Open Championship links and the glorious Surrey courses of Sunningdale, Walton Heath and Wentworth had to be included from the British Isles, as did storied American layouts like the National Golf Links and its Long Island neighbour, Shinnecock Hills; the No. 2 course at Pinehurst in North Carolina; and the fabulous – one is tempted to add the word fabled given the legion of fascinating and fantastic stories to have emerged from it – Pine Valley, in New Jersey, which manages to hold, in the opinion of many experts, the dual honour of being the best golf course in the world and the hardest golf course in the world.

Another course which has been called both those things is Royal Melbourne. The 5th on the West Course, shown on page 120, is also the 5th hole on the Composite Course, which has hosted the Australian Open on 15 occasions.

That, then, is the third group – a group of great courses, with a hole picked from each one which epitomizes its qualities. But it would be inadequate, as well as easy, to stick with the old favourites and neglect the new courses; to hail the work of master course architects like Harry Colt and Dr Alister Mackenzie and to avoid delivering potentially invidious verdicts on their successors of the current generation.

The book seeks instead to present an appropriate blend of the old and the new, a mixture of the revered classics and their respected contemporaries. On the other hand, reviled may be a more accurate adjective than respected in a few cases, notably Pete Dye's creations at PGA West in California and at the Tournament Players Club, headquarters of the American PGA Tour, in Florida. The complete collection of tour players' tributes to PGA West could be fitted on a ball marker. An idea of what they think can be gleaned from the text on page 94. The older TPC has come to be regarded as a kind of genial grandfather in comparison, and, almost perversely, many of those who castigated it as unfair when it opened now feel that it has been softened up too much from the days when it was said by one writer that 'there are enough bad lies to blow the circuits of a polygraph'. Perhaps this only goes to show that it is always going to be hard for modern course architects to compete with history, although Robert Trent Jones Jnr (whose father of the same name has been the most influential designer of the post-war years) has heard little but praise for his layout at Spanish Bay in California, and Jack Nicklaus's first venture into Britain, at St Mellion in Cornwall, has predominantly been applauded.

Across the world, Nicklaus's Desert Highlands in Arizona demonstrates how man can contrive a golf course out of anything, while the 12th hole at La Paz, two miles up in the Bolivian Andes, shows how he can build one anywhere. Man's quest for places to play the game will not be deterred by the quirks of nature. And as Pete Dye realized, to Joe Walser's cost, he will not be put off by a substantial pain in the pocket.

Finally, following the new courses, there is a fifth group to be considered under these broad headings – the resort courses, such as Casa de Campo in the Caribbean, Princeville in Hawaii, Vale do Lobo in Portugal and Waterville in Ireland. They represent another significant aspect of golf course design, and the holes selected to represent them here deserve their inclusion.

While this book primarily depends on the pictorial content for its impact – to present the extraordinary and the extravagant, the special and the spectacular – the words attempt to embellish appreciation of the photographs, either with anecdotes or by description, though obviously the history of the 13th at Augusta National is somewhat richer than that of the 12th at La Paz. Equally obviously, there are references in the copy which require some brief explanation.

An apposite place to start is with the term 'links'. There is a great deal of confusion surrounding the evolution of the word; enough to fill a thin thesaurus and most of it not sufficiently relevant to delve too deeply into here. However, in essence one can regard a links as a golf course built on the stretches of sandy ground left behind by the seas as they receded following the last Ice Age. The grasses which were eventually nurtured upon that land have since provided the territory for what today we call golf links, of which St Andrews is the quintessential example. Technically, depending on one's definition, a links need not be close to the sea and, teasingly, a golf course that is beside the sea may not be a links. Pebble Beach fits into the latter category (it does not lie upon sandy subsoil), while several inland courses in Britain particularly, such as Woodhall Spa in Lincolnshire, possess the basic characteristics of a links if not the heritage. But either on the coast or away from it, it has been one of our blessings that the land which is least suitable for agriculture is the best for golf. The farmer prefers loam, the golfer wants a sand-based turf.

The book also refers regularly to players, both professionals and amateurs, who have performed some notable deed at the hole in question or made some noteworthy comment about it. These golfers are listed in an index on page 160.

And then there are events; the championships and tournaments at which the players establish their reputations. The nature of most events is self-explanatory from the context in which they appear, but a few points may be pertinent at this juncture.

Four golf tournaments stand above the rest: the Open Championship (sometimes, albeit inaccurately, called the 'British Open', especially in America, to distinguish it more clearly from other Opens – a practice I have sometimes adopted here in order to avoid confusion); the United States Open Championship; the Masters Tournament; and the United States PGA Championship. The Open is the oldest championship in golf, founded in 1860, and it is organized by the Royal & Ancient Golf Club of St Andrews (R & A). The US Open, started in 1895, is run by the United States Golf Association (USGA). The PGA Championship is considered, almost universally, to be the least prestigious of the four and ostensibly it has its status under threat from the US PGA Tour's Players Championship, the game's 'fifth major'. The PGA Championship was inaugurated in 1916 and is controlled by the Professional Golfers' Association of America. These three tournaments are held at a host of different venues in their respective countries – although the Open is only played on the links courses of the British Isles – whereas since its inception in 1934 the Masters has always been played at the Augusta National Golf Club.

These four events constitute the modern 'Grand Slam'. Nobody has ever won all four in the same year, and they probably never will, but the concept has existed since Bobby Jones completed the original Grand Slam by winning the British and US Opens and the British and US Amateur Championships in 1930. As the emphasis of the sport has moved increasingly towards professional golf, the two Amateurs have come to be replaced by the Masters and the PGA Championship. The two Amateur Championships remain in existence, of course, and to win one of these titles represents the pinnacle of accomplishment in the non-paid ranks.

Then there are the team competitions: notably the biennial men's professional confrontation for the Ryder Cup between the United States and Europe (it was Great Britain and Ireland until 1979, by which time the Americans had got terminally bored with winning too easily); the men's amateur equivalent between the United States and Great Britain and Ireland for the Walker Cup; the Curtis Cup, again biennially, between the women amateur golfers of the same two nations; the Dunhill Cup, an annual match-format contest between three-man professional teams of many countries; and the World Cup, an annual strokeplay competition involving two-man professional teams, also from many countries. Finally, two other bodies should be mentioned: the United States PGA Tour and the PGA European Tour, which run the lucrative, seasonal professional tournament circuits for their respective geographical areas.

In conclusion, I should like to thank all the clubs featured in the book for their co-operation, particularly in confirming design details of the holes depicted here; and to thank Jeanne Goldstone at *Golf World* for nagging some of them until they did co-operate. I am also indebted to John Robertson, the publishers of *Golf World*, who had the original idea for this book. These holes are extracted from courses that run from one of the finest in the New World, Augusta National, to one of the finest in the Old World, Woodhall Spa. What a 72-hole tournament could be played over them.

Robert Green

London   May 1989

13

13th at Augusta National

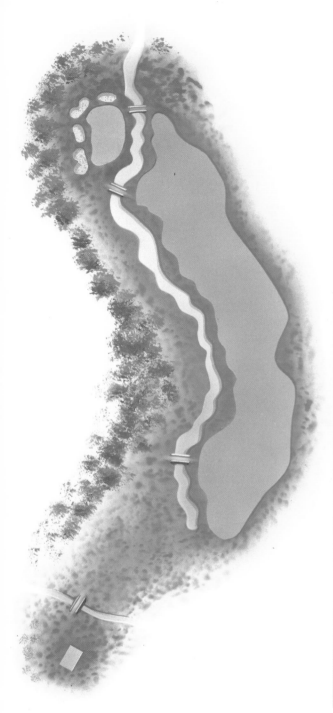

465 YARDS, PAR-5

THE SECOND SHOT to the 13th at Augusta National: the second shot to the 13th at the Masters. The venue and the tournament are, uniquely, almost synonymous. The course was designed by Dr Alister Mackenzie, a Scotsman who also built other magnificent layouts like Cypress Point in California and Royal Melbourne in Australia, in collabora-

tion with the great Bobby Jones after the latter had retired from competitive golf following his completion of the Grand Slam in 1930. Jones himself chose the site at Augusta, in his home state of Georgia.

The Masters, which began in 1934, has become established as the third most prestigious title in the world. Like the club, it is an exclusive affair – entrance by invitation only. The 13th is one of several genuinely

outstanding and beautiful holes at Augusta. In the Scottish tradition it bears a name, 'Azalea', many of which decorate the hillside behind the green. And though Augusta has inspired the creation of thousands of inferior courses around the world, it has also broken some of golf's cherished customs. It is normal for a par-5 to measure over 475 yards, but not in this case. Yet this hole is one of the most renowned and revered long holes in golf. Japan's Tsuneyuki (Tommy) Nakajima once took 13 here. The drive has to reach the angle in the sharp dog-leg left in order to give the golfer any hope of getting home in two, and if he is tempted to go for it there is a creek running down the left side of the fairway and in front of the green which may dissuade him.

Countless times the destiny of the Masters has been decided in the waters of the 13th, the last of a three-hole stretch known as 'Amen Corner'. In 1937 Ralph Guldahl took six here; Byron Nelson made three. Nelson won by two strokes. In 1954 the amateur Billy Joe Patton led by one until he suffered a seven. He missed a playoff by a shot. In 1985 Curtis Strange seemed well in command until a six on the 13th rocked him and let in Bernhard Langer. So it goes on, and so it always will.

11th at Ballybunion (Old Course)

B ALLYBUNION HAS ONE of the best links golf courses in the world, and now that its wonderful Old Course has a worthy companion in the New the club can certainly boast of having the best 36 holes of links golf anywhere. This arresting view of the approach shot to the 11th should help to explain why. The eminent American golf writer and author, Herbert Warren Wind, referred to Ballybunion as 'the finest seaside course I have ever seen'. One of his countrymen, who has a bit of a reputation as a player, judged it to be 'a course on which architects should live and play before they build golf courses'. That was Tom Watson, who has been known to take double advantage of his visits to the British Isles each July by arranging a game over Ballybunion's great links either the week before or after the Open Championship.

Wind described the 11th as 'another dazzling cliffside hole' (there is more than one at Ballybunion) and as 'a perfect beauty'. There isn't a bunker on it, but who needs sand on a hole of this quality when there is a golden expanse of beach ready to greet either a pushed drive or second shot?

This photograph is taken from approx-

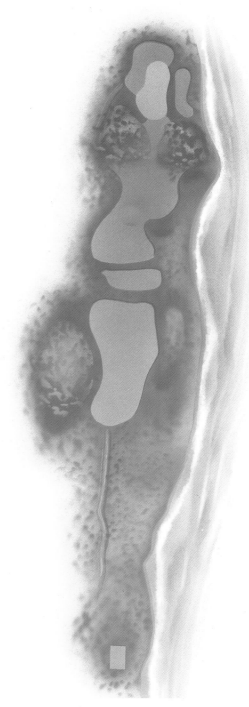

imately the spot where a decent drive will finish. A mid-iron is called for now, but nowhere in the British Isles is more exacting than Ballybunion in the premium it places on the accuracy and trueness of strike required in one's approach play. The 11th epitomizes those virtues. The rugged sandhills protect the flag as if it were a precious jewel, and the green is upraised on a small plateau and thus tends to throw off an indifferent shot. This corner of Co. Kerry contains the best collection of courses in Ireland, but Ballybunion Old stands supreme among them. Although it is tucked away in the far south-west of the Irish Republic, it is besieged by thousands of visitors from around the world each year.

4th at Baltusrol (Lower Course)

192 YARDS, PAR-3

NOT MANY MEN have a golf course named after them, and Mr Baltus Roll would doubtless have preferred not to be an exception to the rule. He was the New Jersey farmer who was murdered in 1825 on the land where Baltusrol Golf Club now stands in the northern part of that state.

In its original form the club hosted two US Opens. It was then expanded between the wars to accommodate two first-class layouts, and the Upper Course staged the 1936 championship. The Lower has since entertained three US Opens, the latter two – in 1967 and 1980 – both being won by Jack Nicklaus. On each occasion he made a birdie four on the 18th, which winds towards the stately clubhouse in the left-hand portion of this picture, to establish a new record total

for the 72 holes of the championship.

But it is the 4th which is Baltusrol's most celebrated hole. It is not a great strategic hole because there is only one way to play it. If you do not clear the water, you have to tee up another ball and try again. The bunkers at the back await an over-bold or over-cautious tee shot, and from there the explosion shot back is an extremely nervy affair. The green is wide enough to gather a ball struck a little off line, but it is so shallow that it is imperative to choose the correct club. This particular hole is the work of Robert Trent Jones, the doyen of contemporary golf course architects, who was brought in by officials at Baltusrol to modify the course for the 1954 US Open. When he had finished the job, it was suggested that he had made the 4th too tough even for the professionals. Jones went out with the club pro (former US Open champion, Johnny Farrell), the club president and the chairman of the championship committee, put down a ball and holed out in one – a pretty emphatic way of rebuffing his critics.

8th at Banff Springs

T HAS BEEN SAID that to suggest that the Banff Springs Golf Club is blessed with one of the most geographically stupendous settings in the world is to do it less than justice. Out of this world is often the favoured expression. The Canadian Rockies loom in the distance, the mountain peaks tipped with snow virtually all the year round. A

game of golf in the bracing environment of Alberta, in the heady air 5000 feet above sea level, is an experience to savour. Its remoteness is one of Banff's many attractions, but it has to be acknowledged that it is only because of man's advances in engineering that the natural landscape of the area has been able to be rearranged (i.e. blasted and quarried) into the shape necessary to produce such a spectacular golf course.

The 8th is a case in point. It demands fine judgment to pick the correct club for the tee shot on this hole and considerable nerve to execute the shot in the desired fashion. From the elevated tee in the distance it is easy to succumb to the temptation to take a club or two too much in order to clear the glacial lake, an error all the easier to make if the golfer is confused by the gentle breezes swirling over the water

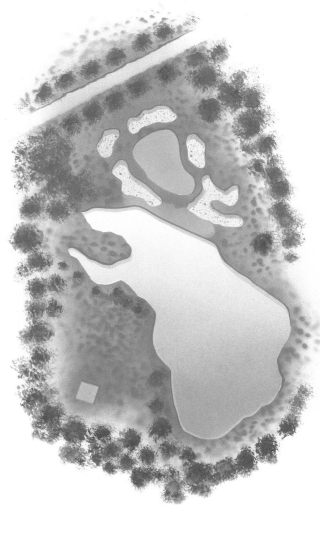

from the adjacent mountains. The consequences of over-clubbing generally involve a hunt for the ball in the forest over the back of the green. The consequences of being short involve playing three off the tee. At least the hillside into which the green is cut tends to throw the ball towards the pin – always assuming that it hasn't found one of the encircling bunkers in the meantime.

The 8th at Banff is known as the 'Devil's Cauldron', which aptly indicates the hole's degree of difficulty and yet seems slightly incongruous in such blissful surroundings. But then it is one of golf's abundant charms that many of its hazards, such as these firs and the lake, not only attract the golfer's ball but the eye as well.

17th at Bay Hill

223 YARDS, PAR-3

THIS DAUNTING PAR-3 is the centrepiece of Bay Hill's exacting finish, sandwiched as it is between two long, water-strewn par-4s. There are in fact 27 holes at Bay Hill, but when the toughest 18 are selected each spring for Bay Hill's annual appearance on the US PGA Tour the organizers can come up with a stiff test for the professionals which measures over 7100 yards from the back.

The 17th is an excellent example of the archetypal Florida hole. The land is almost invariably flat, so it is to the gleaming white bunkers and the deep blue water hazards that the course must look for both distinction and means of defence. The problems posed by the shot in hand are all too evident. It requires a hefty blow with a long club in order to make the carry across the

lake, and even a dry landing provides no guarantee that one's next effort will not have to be a splash shot from the sand. The 'official' strategy here is to ignore the location of the pin and instead play for the left-centre portion of the green, irrespective of where the flag is. An annotation on the scorecard pulls no punches in its declaration as to the merits of the 17th. It reads: 'This hole is rated as one of the best par-3s in the world. Par here is a great score!'

Bay Hill is in central Florida, at Orlando, and Arnold Palmer maintains a home there, as do hundreds of other Americans in what is one of the nation's great holiday golf regions. The course was originally designed by Dick Wilson, an esteemed golf course architect, but Palmer has subsequently made the odd change here and there. He rates the 17th as one of his favourite holes

anywhere. It is surely one of American tour pro Don Pooley's favourites, too. At the 1987 Bay Hill Classic, he holed his tee shot with a 4-iron, an ace that was worth $500,000 to him and the same amount to a local hospital.

18th at The Belfry (Brabazon Course)

455 YARDS, PAR-4

THE BELFRY IS UGLY. It is not a good golf course. Well, those are two statements frequently uttered in discussions about the West Midlands complex near Birmingham, England's second largest city. Perhaps this shot from behind the 18th green on the Brabazon Course will go some way towards dismissing the former claim, although na-

ture will play a greater part in doing that when the young trees and bushes around the Brabazon Course have had the chance to mature and flourish. As to the playing merits of the layout, the course has already proved to the best golfers in the world that it cannot be trifled with.

The Belfry is the home of the British Professional Golfers' Association. The latter body organizes the biennial Ryder Cup

match between Europe and the United States when every four years it is played in Britain. That is why The Belfry was awarded the 1985 match. The on-course success of the European team on that occasion, the first time in 28 years that the Americans had been defeated, just may have had something to do with the return of the contest to The Belfry in 1989.

The 18th – not surprisingly in a match-play confrontation – proved to be crucial. The United States led until the last hole of the second morning's fourballs, when Craig Stadler missed a straight uphill putt from 18 inches to allow Europe to draw level. Duly buoyed, the Europeans won three of the four afternoon foursomes and the next day won four and halved one of the six singles which went to the home green. Ray Floyd handed victory to Paul Way when his second shot from a fairway bunker found the water in front of this green. Europe's triumph was secured when the US Open champion, Andy North, drove into the lake from the 18th tee and left Sam Torrance the pleasure of holing from 18 feet for the clinching birdie with the pressure removed. But The Belfry emerged as a champion as well. Even in winning, the European team was an estimated cumulative 23 over par for the 12 singles.

15th at Carnoustie

GARY PLAYER is not a man inclined to use the positive when there is a superlative available, but his description of Carnoustie as 'the toughest golf course in the world' is not considered to be one of his wilder statements. When protected by the customary wind off the Tay estuary, Carnoustie can torment the most gifted exponents of the game. It measures over 7000 yards from the championship tees, and never do more than two consecutive holes run in the same direction.

It is a sore point indeed around that part of Angus that the championship tees on what is undisputably one of Scotland's great links have not been employed as often as the locals would like lately. Five Open Championships have been held at Carnous-

tie, but none since 1975. Its champions have all been of the highest calibre – Tommy Armour (1931), Henry Cotton (1937), Ben Hogan (1953), Gary Player (1968) and Tom Watson (1975) – so nobody can cast aspersions as to the quality of the course. Instead it is doubts as to whether Carnoustie could cope with the extraneous necessities of the modern Open, like accommodation, that have kept the championship away.

It would be a terrible shame if the Open never returned to Carnoustie. Holes like the 15th deserve to pit their nuances against the skills of the best. It was on the 15th during the second round in 1975 that Peter Oosterhuis, then the championship leader, began a damaging run of three successive bogeys; here, too, on the final day that Watson missed the first of three consecutive putts from inside 10 feet which seemed certain to enhance his then reputation as a man who would always find a way to lose. A birdie at the last and a 71 to Jack Newton's 72 in the playoff the next day altered all that.

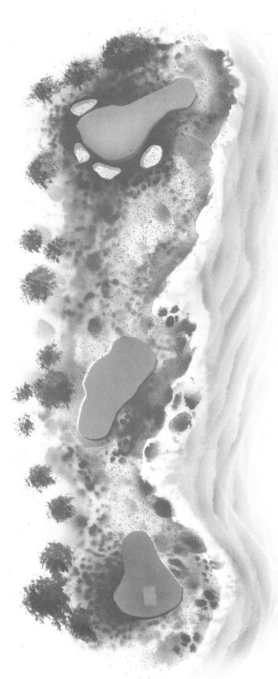

185 YARDS, PAR-3

N POSSIBLY HIS MOST outstanding achievement, Pete Dye, who is responsible for a number of courses included here, constructed this beautiful and remarkable layout from a jungle near La Romana in the Dominican Republic. Today that former in-hospitable wilderness has been replaced by what is recognized as the best course in the Caribbean. Inland it weaves its way between coconut, citrus and cashew trees, but the splendour of those holes is almost reduced to the prosaic by the spectacular majesty of the two sequences of four holes along the ocean: from the 5th to the 8th and from the 14th to the 17th.

This is the 16th hole, one of four breathtaking par-3s on the Teeth of the Dog, an arcane-sounding name derived from a

translation of the Spanish term (*dientes del perro*) for the type of indigenous jagged coral used to buttress several features on the course, like the tees on this hole. That sort of attention to detail is only proper given the back-breaking toil undertaken by the 300-strong Dominican labour force which cleared the site with machetes, and given the persistence of the property owner who nagged Dye until he agreed to tackle the job with the thought: 'Well, he's got 300,000 acres. There must be a golf course out there somewhere.' These days, as one can see, there is an airstrip, too.

Despite his initial reluctance, Dye has created a masterpiece. Holes such as the 16th ineluctably lead to comparisons between Casa de Campo and Pebble Beach in California. In fact, although this course cannot boast a dramatic beach-side finale to match that at Pebble, it has more, and arguably better, shoreline holes. The eight here occupy over three miles of this Caribbean coastline and, unlike Pebble Beach, the golfer frequently has no choice but to play his ball over the surf. The 16th makes the point emphatically. One is either on the green or in serious trouble. But if one has to end up in bunkers, trees, sea or sand, this is a most exquisite place in which to do it.

8th at Chantilly

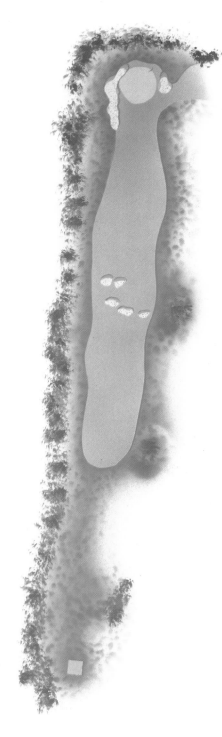

577 YARDS, PAR-5

SOME 20 MILES north of the gracious city of Paris lies the gracious town of Chantilly, the Gallic headquarters of thoroughbred horse racing and a place immortalized for millions of non-French people in the song 'Chantilly Lace'. And the golf course here, overall probably the best in France, presents such a pretty face, too, with the avenues of fairway which run between the splendid trees seeming, at first sight, to be as broad and spacious as the Champs Elysées. But first impressions can be misleading. Serious trouble is never too far from the straight and deceptively narrow. And when Chantilly hosts the French Open Championship, its fairways are tightened and its rough is heightened. Nick Faldo, then the reigning British Open champion,

was victorious at Chantilly in 1988, which, given his reputation as an excellent player of tough courses, enhanced the course's reputation as well as his own.

The Chantilly we know today was redesigned by the esteemed and sometimes irascible English golf course architect Tom Simpson, who once tried to pressurize a golf club committee into giving him the job of providing their new layout by driving his Rolls-Royce back and forth in front of their window while they were considering their decision. Invariably, awarding the contract to Simpson was a good idea. One of his moves here was to reduce the number of bunkers. But, as this picture shows, he did not make those he left any less severe.

These formidable fairway bunkers are sited some 340 yards from the back tee, although they can easily come into play if one of the three sets of forward markers is used. A sprawling bunker guards the left side of the green, making the flag – when it is in this position – only accessible by an approach shot of about 240 yards, drawn in from the right. More sand on that side of the green means that only a perfectly executed and powerfully struck shot will suffice. This is one long hole where to make five is no disgrace.

1st at Cherry Hills

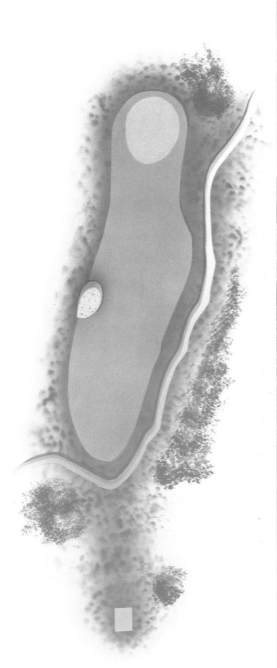

346 YARDS, PAR-4

IT IS NOT OFTEN that the first hole of a golf course can justifiably claim to have witnessed the critical moment in a championship or tournament, but that is what happened at Cherry Hills in the final round of the 1960 US Open.

Arnold Palmer walked onto the tee seven strokes behind the leader, Mike Souchak. On this seemingly innocuous par-4, he had respectively taken six, five and four in the first three rounds. That was the price Palmer had paid for trying to drive the green in order to give himself the chance of making an eagle two. In the rarefied air of the Colorado Rockies just outside Denver, such a policy was not ridiculous – the ball flies further at altitude. It was simply that Palmer's execution had been terrible. Now

that he was seven shots adrift there was clearly no point in playing safe off the tee with an iron and being content with a pitch to the green, which would be the aim for mere mortals. Out came the driver again, but this time the ball finished on the green. Palmer did not hole the putt for his eagle but he made a three and then proceeded to birdie five of the next six holes as well. That set him up for a closing 65, good enough for

him to claim the title with two shots to spare. Later he reflected: 'Not until that summer day in 1960 did it become apparent to me how boldness might influence not just a hole but an entire round, an entire tournament, and even an entire golfing career.'

That was Cherry Hills' second US Open. Its third was in 1978, when Andy North got up and down in two shots from a bunker at the last for a bogey five to win by a stroke.

North triumphed despite failing to hit the first green in two, let alone in one, in the final round. For that matter, he didn't hit any of the first three greens in regulation figures, but he saved his par every time. Earlier, Tom Watson, who had started the day eight shots behind, had birdied the first three holes, but it was to no avail. It has never been easy to follow in Arnie's footsteps.

9th at Chung Shan Hot Spring

THE SOVIET UNION EXPECTS to have its first golf course early in the 1990s. In that respect at least it is behind its great Communist rival, China. The Chung Shan course in Guandong province, an hour from Hong Kong by hovercraft, was designed by Arnold Palmer, who in his more renowned role as a professional golfer was almost single-handedly responsible for showing the American public in the 1960s what a thrilling game golf could be. While Palmer was revelling in his glory days on the US tour, golf was banned in Red China. That prohibition followed the People's Revolution of 1949. The golf courses were turned into paddy fields; one of capitalism's arch-pastimes was banished.

That all changed with the demise of Chairman Mao Tse-Tung and the gradual Chinese embrace of Western mores. Chung Shan was opened in 1984, 1500 workers having been employed to undertake the construction. In this age when man often spares no expense and utilizes the most advanced technology simply to build a golf course in most areas of the world, the Chinese labourers had to do it all by hand. But now the locals, not merely voyeuristic

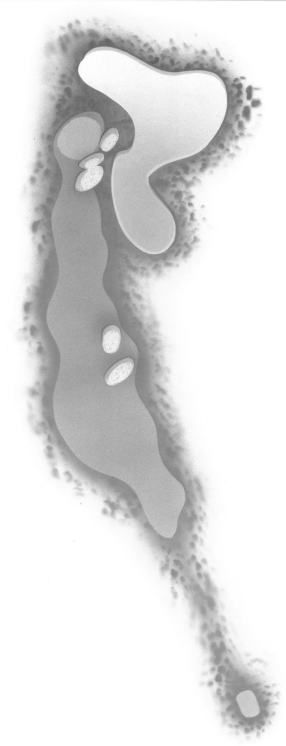

398 YARDS, PAR-4

foreigners such as American and Japanese business executives and adventurous tourists, have reaped the pleasures of playing the game. In a manner evocative of East Germany, potential golfers were selected from young native students and within three years of being introduced to the game they were breaking par round Chung Shan – from not knowing what golf was to not knowing, apparently, how difficult it is. They evidently even managed to cope with the perils of the 9th, where the water-threatened approach shot is perhaps the most demanding of any on the course.

Chung Shan was the first post-Revolution course in the country, but already the total is in double figures and mounting. The 9th at Chung Shan is of an apposite shape. It, like the nation's politics have, bends gently to the right.

5th at Colonial

THE COLONIAL COUNTRY CLUB AT Fort Worth in Texas was once described by former US Open and Masters champion Cary Middlecoff as having 'the toughest par-70 course in the world'. At 7116 yards, it is not hard to imagine what Middlecoff meant. This hole, the 5th, is generally regarded as the hardest of the lot. One American commenta-tor has called it perhaps 'the most difficult par-4 on earth'; another has ranked it as the best 5th hole in the United States.

The ideal strategy is to hit a powerful fade with the driver in order to negotiate the gentle curve to the right off the tee. This will leave a long iron, or maybe even a wood, into the green. The tree-lines on either edge of the fairway stress the importance of accuracy, and the Trinity River on the right side and a shallow ditch on the left lie waiting to penalize the errant golfer still further. In the only US Open to be held at Colonial, in 1941 (the first ever in the American South), Craig Wood's drive at this hole in the second round went into the ditch. His back was causing him great pain, there was thunder and lightning raging all around the course, and he was three over par for the championship and felt he had

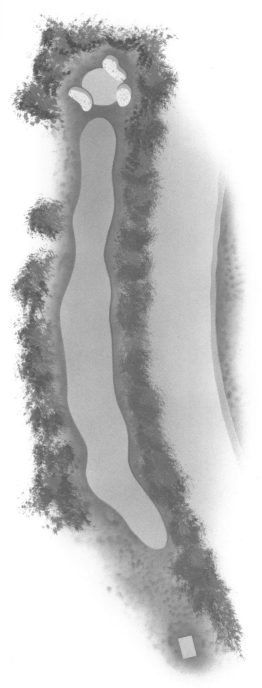

466 YARDS, PAR-4

blown his chances of victory. He told his playing partner, Tommy Armour, that he was packing in. Armour dissuaded him from doing that and, though Wood bogeyed the 5th, he played the next 49 holes in level par and won by three shots from his long-time rival, Denny Shute.

Ben Hogan honed his skills at Colonial in his formative years, and he would later confess that being familiar with such a demanding golf course enabled him to handle better the lesser challenges posed elsewhere. Even a man with Hogan's ability could not guarantee to make four on the 5th every day.

17th at Cypress Point

PEBBLE BEACH, on California's Monterey Peninsula, is unique in the world of golf in boasting two courses – Cypress Point and Pebble Beach itself – that are included in most listings of the finest ten courses on the planet. A large part of their spectacular charm is due to the unsurpassable beauty of the topography of the coastline. As the writer Cal Brown has noted: 'There cannot be another place on earth quite like it. It is as though every thundering emotion, every subtle line, had been withheld from the rest of creation and then dumped in one place to test our understanding of the superlative.'

Among the tributes showered upon Cypress Point in particular is one from Sandy Tatum, a member who is also a former president of the US Golf Association. He calls it 'the Sistine Chapel of Golf'. Slightly less complimentary is the comment that Cypress is the best 17-hole golf course in the world, a reference to its relatively lacklustre closing hole. If the purists had their way, Cypress Point would finish here, on the beautiful 17th, one of the sort of sights that prompted Bobby Jones's biographer, O. B Keeler, to note that the whole place resembled 'the crystallization of the

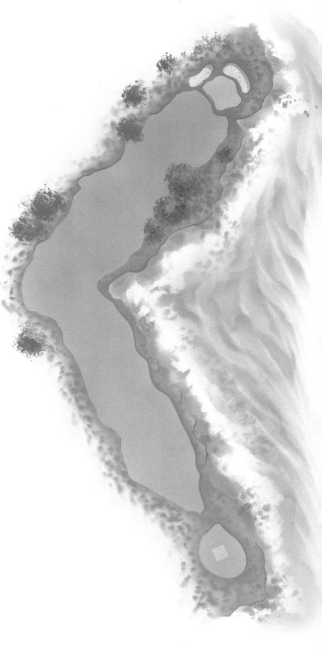

dream of an artist who had been drinking gin and sobering up on absinthe'.

Once one has conquered the potentially ruinous mixture of appreciation of the setting and apprehension of the task in hand, it is time to address the tee shot. The cluster of gnarled cypress trees define the target area, but only with a howling gale behind off the Pacific is it worth trying to cut too much length off the hole. On the other hand, a shot played over the narrower part of the bay will leave the golfer with a long iron or maybe a wood in his hands if he is to reach the green in two, and anything not driven firmly enough will find the player blocked out from a direct line into the flag by those same cypresses. The 17th is a beauty alright, but it can be a beast.

1st at Desert Highlands

356 YARDS, PAR-4

THE OPTIONS HERE ARE evidently limited. One is either on the carpet or among the cacti. As the name suggests, most of the sand at Desert Highlands was provided not by man but by the Almighty. The opening hole is a classic of the genre. The targets, both fairway and green, are big enough, but they can seem to shrink to the size of a handkerchief once one has taken in the obvious penalties of being wayward. Seldom can the wisdom of the old, oft-repeated golfing adage about keeping the ball straight down the middle have been more explicitly demonstrated.

Desert Highlands, at Scottsdale in Arizona, is a classic example of the way man has employed the advances in technology to create something beautiful out of some-

thing barren. Today we have the machines that can drain marshes and, in this instance, irrigate these emerald oases in the desert. The fairways are effectively turned up at the edges so as not to waste the precious resource of water by pouring it onto the wasteland.

This course is just one of the many that have recently been nurtured in apparent defiance of nature from the Arizona desert; indeed, nature has been here used to blend the bunkers into the environment. In addition to offering a spectacular view of the green ribbon of fairway and of the arid, rugged landscape beyond, the first tee at Desert Highlands also affords a sight of the fact that makes such developments possible – the holiday homes which play an integral part in financing the project. In the case of Desert Highlands, there was a help-ful publicity boost to begin with. The course was the venue for the inaugural televised Skins Game between four of the greats – Jack Nicklaus, Arnold Palmer, Gary Player and Tom Watson – in 1983.

9th at El Saler

SEVE BALLESTEROS spotted a struggling English professional after he had completed his first round in the 1984 Spanish Open over Javier Arana's finest golf course creation, El Saler, near Valencia. 'How did you do?' asked the great Spaniard. 'Not bad', came the reply, 'a 68.' 'Not bad', exclaimed Ballesteros with vehemence. 'You think peo-

ple will shoot 65 round here?' In fact, another prominent Spaniard, Manuel Pinero, did just that in the final round, and his achievement was all but ignored. Behind him, Bernhard Langer was compiling a score which is still spoken of with awe on the European tour, a round which Langer regards as the best of his career even though he has subsequently won the Masters at Augusta. Using only 25 putts, Langer re-

corded ten birdies – including nine in 11 holes from the 5th – and eight pars to shoot an incredible 62 and win the title which ensured he would top the European Money List (Order of Merit) for the second time.

The 9th was one of the holes which fell to Langer's onslaught. As the shortest hole on a course measuring over 7000 yards, that is perhaps not surprising, but El Saler is not just about length. Its 9th hole is all about

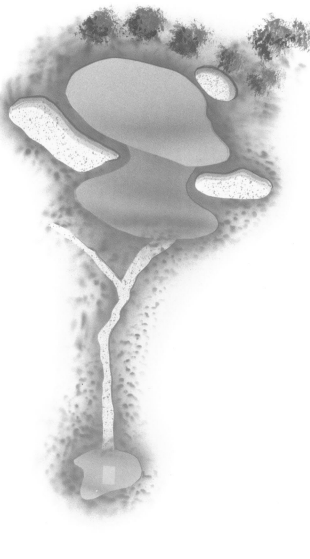

accuracy. The cavernous bunkers short, left and right of the green are likely to induce a fatal tightening of the grip in many a golfer, and anyone taking too much club with the intention of clearing all the trouble is liable to find some more in the hollows of the sparse copse over the back. Holing a 20-foot putt for a two, as Langer did that spectacular day, would be a treat indeed.

The 9th at El Saler is indicative of the course's mixed elements: the atmosphere of a links, as in the proximity of the Mediterranean and the presence of dunes and other sandy scrub, combined with a heathland-cum-forest feel that is prevalent among the sombrero pines on the holes away from the sea. But in either mode, El Saler is a great course and all the greater for proving, as it did in Bernhard Langer's case, that it will bow to brilliance.

18th at Falsterbo

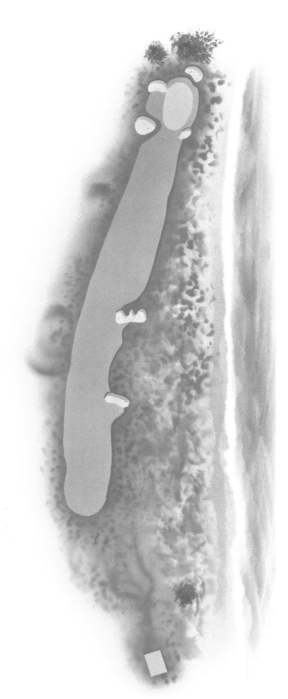

505 YARDS, PAR-5

THE PREMIER GOLF COURSE of Scandinavia is Falsterbo, a genuine links which occupies a superb stretch of sandy flatland just outside the tranquil, picturesque town of Skanör, 30 miles from the major port of Malmö in the far south of Sweden. The long finishing hole epitomizes the perils and the pleasures of golf at Falsterbo, where the rough largely consists of reed grasses nourished by a myriad of natural ponds and where the sand bunkers are plentiful and punitive. These facets of the course are shown here, as are Falsterbo's landmark – the old lighthouse on the horizon to the right – and the primary source of its winds that bedevil and yet beguile the golfer – the Baltic Sea.

The chill air off the sea is tempered in summer by the heat generated throughout

those long, seemingly endless days when the bleakness generally associated with the Baltic gives way to a charm and a wild beauty that are enhanced by the very remoteness of the place and by the regular sight and sound of several species of bird life.

The sort of bird life all golfers are interested in at Falsterbo is that to be found in the satisfaction of making a four on the 18th. Looking back towards the tee, up in the

dunes to the left, it is immediately palpable that a bad slice means a premature visit to the enticing beach, but in the anxiety to keep left many a player will pull the drive into the rough, which makes an already long hole even longer since the fairway cuts away to the right, following the line of the sand-hills, after the driving zone has been reached. Then it is simply straight forward to the green, as long as one is able to hit the

ball straight and forward along the narrow ribbon of fairway between the rough and the dunes, between the devil and the deep blue sea. That is why it is easier to see a birdie on this hole than to make one.

16th at Firestone (South Course)

THIS IS ONE OF THE most recognized holes in golf – the monstrous 16th at the Firestone Country Club in Akron, Ohio, the home for the World Series of Golf every year since its inception in 1962. The event began life as a television spectacular, bringing together the winners of the game's four major championships: the British and US Opens, the Masters and the US PGA Championship. The 16th invariably featured prominently in those early broadcasts and does so no less now that the format of the tournament has been expanded.

Firestone's reputation has been further enhanced by the TV exposure received during the three US PGA Championships held over its formidable 7173-yard, par-70 course, and the 16th has played a notable part on each of those auspicious occasions. In 1960 Arnold Palmer was putting together one of his patented 'charges' when he dunked his ball into the pond with his third shot and shortly afterwards marked an eight on his card, while the pond knocked all the steam out of Sam Snead in 1966 when he was bidding to claim his fourth PGA title at the age of 54. And in 1975 Jack Nicklaus was never again under pressure after blasting a

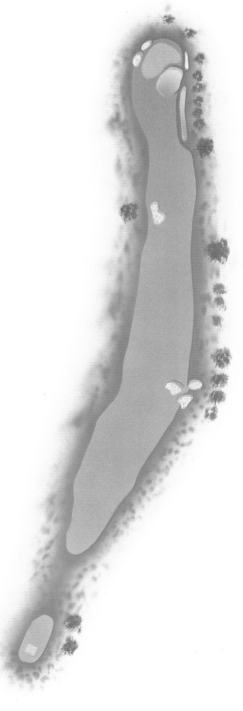

9-iron onto the green from the right rough over the trees in the left of this picture during the third round. He holed the 30-footer he had left for a valiant five and was not seriously challenged further.

Despite its awesome length, the 16th has been reached in two blows by the likes of Palmer and Nicklaus. Even the long hitters of the US circuit cannot do that with any regularity, but the hole does fall downhill from the tee, thus encouraging the mighty to go for the green with their second shots after a perfect drive. But perfect it has to be. That pond has swallowed up many a tentative pitch over the years, so it takes a heroic wood shot to get past it.

5th at Ganton

GANTON IS ONE OF THOSE magnificent English courses which are regularly described as an inland links. This photograph provides the explanation. Ganton is not on the sea, although that is only 10 miles away at Scarborough on the Yorkshire coast, and the sparse trees and flora in the right-hand foreground of the picture are more common sights on an inland course than on a links. The immediate surroundings, of the gentle hills and fields of the Vale of Pickering, confirm that this is a heathland course.

On the other hand, Ganton bears more than a vague resemblance to a genuine links. Some of its bunkers are cavernous; seemingly big enough to accommodate an entire all-exempt tour. Its gorse bushes and rough provide alternative sources of ferocious trouble. The sandy turf affords a wonderful base from which to execute one's approach shots, and it was this quality and Ganton's firm, true greens that Michael Bonallack exploited to such devastating effect in the final of the 1968 English Amateur Championship. Bonallack's brilliance overwhelmed David Kelley by 12 and 11. The man who is now secretary of the R & A shot 61, ten under par, in the morning

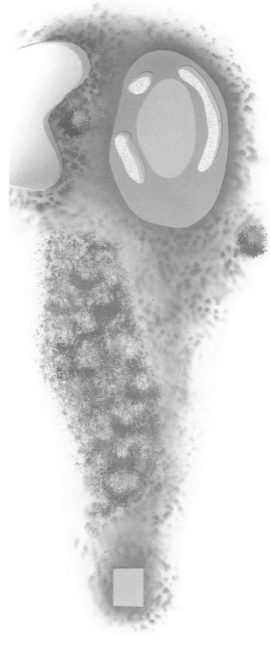

round. He will be looking forward to 1991, when in its centenary season the club will stage the British Amateur for the third time. And if one doubted Ganton's quasi-linksland credentials, one might be convinced by knowing that it is the only non-links course ever to be accorded the honour of hosting that championship.

Not that Ganton has any reason to want to pretend to be anything it isn't. From the days when Harry Vardon, six-time winner of the Open Championship, was the club's professional, it has been a hard, fair and enjoyable test of golf. The 5th epitomizes those values. It is not long, especially since it is played from a raised tee by the hut in the distance, but it is not easy. The green is generous enough, but miss it and those man-sized bunkers await, as does the water for anything very left of perfect.

18th at Gleneagles (King's Course)

ROBABLY MORE THAN ANY OTHER golf club in the British Isles, Gleneagles owes its worldwide reputation to the beauty of its surroundings. There are four 18-hole courses attached to the opulent Gleneagles Hotel at Auchterarder in Perthshire, and two of them – the King's and the Queen's – are of genuine championship quality. Yet it is for the magnificence of its setting that the place is chiefly renowned. It may be the yellow of the gorse in spring or the purple of the heather in summer, or simply the way the gentle sunlight plays upon the hills, the valleys and the trees, but however it does it Gleneagles will captivate you.

Scotland is, obviously, more revered for its matchless collection of links courses than for its inland tests, but Gleneagles, and particularly the King's Course, is the most eminent exception to that rule. The 18th is one of its strongest holes, although it does not play as long as the card suggests because it falls gradually downhill from tee to green. Big hitters like Greg Norman have been known to get home with a drive and a wedge. With a healthy wind behind him, Tom Watson once boomed a tee shot 486 yards from this tee in a pro-celebrity exhibi-

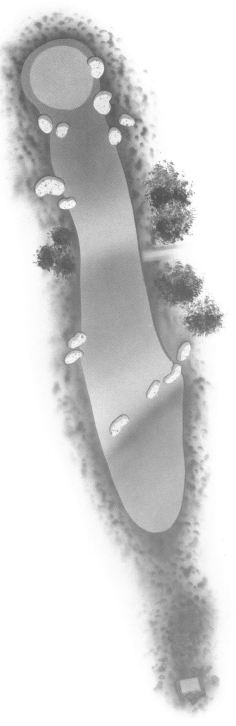

tion. Ironically, one of his opponents on that occasion was none other than Mr. Norman.

From the tee boxes beside the little hut just beyond the 17th green, the drive should ideally clear the crest of the ridge over a line between the twin bunkers. It will then catch a downslope which will speed the ball on towards its ultimate destination. Thereafter, again ideally, the player will repair for the night to the splendour of the hotel in the background. But do not allow this portrait of evening bliss to create a false impression. The King's may be one of the most wonderful courses on earth on which to enjoy the game, but it is not one of the easiest.

7th at Grand Cypress (South Course)

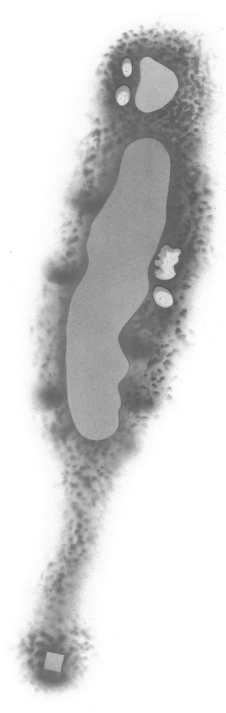

432 YARDS, PAR-4

F YOU THINK this looks like Britain then Jack Nicklaus has succeeded admirably in his task. This is not, in fact, Royal Dornoch. It is, instead, Grand Cypress. It is not the natural rolling duneland of north-east Scotland but the unremitting flatland of central Florida.

Grand Cypress is only open to guests of the Hyatt Regency Hotel at Orlando and, as with his work at Desert Highlands, Nicklaus has set a high standard in another aspect of American contemporary course architecture – hotel golf, though to describe Grand Cypress merely as a hotel track would be as misleading and as inadequate as calling St Andrews a seaside course.

Grand Cypress illustrates how a big budget can stretch to enabling the work of

God to be altered by man; how the indigenous landscape can be substantially reshuffled. The use of 'chocolate drop' and cone-shaped mounds has become something of a Nicklaus trademark, one which some purists dislike but nevertheless a practice which has here created at least a resemblance to a British links. This hole typifies the occasional American obsession to go to great cost in an attempt to capture what is rather perversely termed 'the natural look'. Despite the wild grasses and the gentle undulations of the fairway, this is not the real thing. Apart from other considerations, the sand is too white and the sun too bright in Florida, but the golf need be no less enjoyable for that. In 1988, Nicklaus unveiled another design of his at Grand Cypress – an 18-hole layout modelled on the Old Course at St Andrews. The famous, or the infamous, 17th has been reshaped to accommodate a fade (the patented Nicklaus shot), rather than a draw as in Scotland. The sublime to the ridiculous, or the sublime to the subliminal?

13th at Hamburger

T IS QUITE EASY for even a gifted player to make a meal of the Hamburger Golf Club, but most of the time the prospect of tackling it is anticipated with relish. This glorious German course just outside Hamburg is better known as Falkenstein and, for those who intend to devour it, it provides ample food for thought.

This view from behind the 13th green emphasizes both Falkenstein's menace and its magnificence. The drive is launched from out of a tree-lined chute, and the ideal portion of the fairway is not an easy target to shoot at. The hole is not long anyway, and the fact that it is played from an elevated tee means that it plays shorter still, but the dog-leg to the left is quite a sharp one and the tee shot has to be decently struck and

demonstrably accurate if the pitch to the green is to be as simple as the card would indicate. The 13th is typical of the course: sparsely bunkered dog-legs are Falkenstein's forte (this hole only has two bunkers on it, on the right side of the fairway and the right front edge of the green) and majestic pines and birch are present in profusion.

Falkenstein has been a frequent host to the German Open, and it was fitting that the

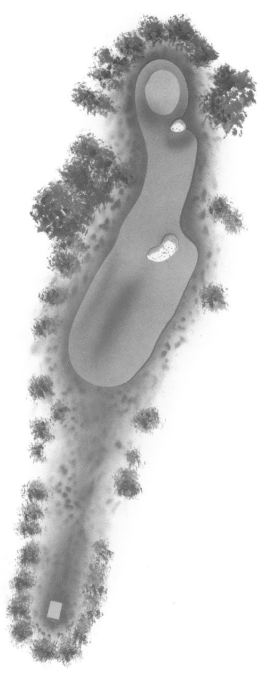

1981 championship there should be won by Bernhard Langer. To the German public, it was hardly unexpected. Two weeks previously Langer had come second in the British Open at Royal St George's, where he had been asked 'Who is the best golfer Germany has ever produced?' A blushingly reluctant Langer had answered: 'I think that must be myself.'. After that statement he was under some pressure at Falkenstein, but he proved then that he was right as he has many times since. In achieving all his accomplishments despite the immense weight of national expectation which will always fall on those who are effectively their country's sole representative in any field, Langer has encouraged the youth of Germany to take up golf, and more courses of the calibre of Falkenstein may be built as a consequence.

18th at Harbour Town

A T THE BEGINNING of autumn 1968, the golf course at Harbour Town on Hilton Head Island, South Carolina, did not exist. At the beginning of November 1969, it had been opened. By the end of the month, it had staged its first US PGA Tour event – the Heritage Classic. The winner was Arnold Palmer. Harbour Town has thus progressed

rapidly from its original state as a wilderness to its current status as one of the finest golf courses in the United States. That transformation is a tribute to its creator, Pete Dye.

Dye built Harbour Town with small, flat greens, wide fairways and few bunkers. At 6657 yards it is comparatively short by modern standards, but it is manifestly no pushover. Nowhere is that made more plain

than on the finishing hole. The tee shot, played from just to the left of the 17th green in the foreground, has to carry one stretch of water to reach the safe promontory of the fairway, or else flirt with the out-of-bounds on the right. It was fear of hitting his drive so far that it would carry into the next, second stretch of water that led Steve Jones to ease up with his final tee shot in the 1987 Heritage Classic. As a result, he blocked his

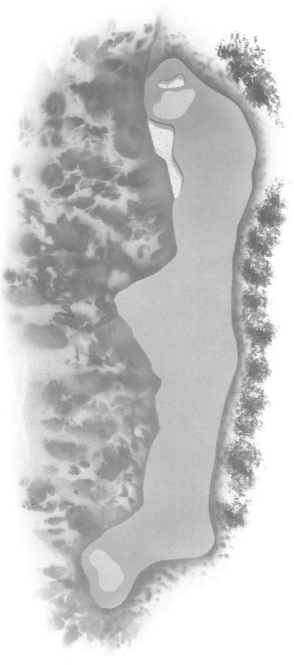

ball out-of-bounds and eventually holed out for a six. It was an extremely costly error. A four would have brought him his first US tour victory. Instead, the pleasure of that achievement went to the beneficiary of Jones's blunder, Davis Love III.

A further expanse of the Calibogue Sound, the section that Jones was worried about, then has to be cleared by the golfer intent on getting home in two. Calibogue is

pronounced 'Cali-bogey', and it has caused many a double-bogey and worse. And if the marshy waters don't get you, that ample greenside bunker might. The safe line with the approach is to aim at the distinctive red and white hooped lighthouse and hope to get up and down with a pitch and a putt for a four. As with most great holes, there is more than one way to play it. For most of us, that is as a par-5.

7th at Hills of Lakeway

THE HILLS OF LAKEWAY course on Lake Travis, a salubrious estate complex some 25 minutes drive from downtown Austin in central Texas, is the third Jack Nicklaus-designed golf course to be included thus far and it epitomizes yet another trend in American course architecture: the inclination to opt for the extravagant flourish.

It goes without saying that the natural limestone waterfall is very much in play. This is not a par-3 on which to be short, although the prospect of over-hitting into one of the bunkers and then facing a trap shot back to the long but shallow green and towards the waters of Hurst Creek is not a great deal more appealing. Playing ultra-safe from the tee, into the hillside, is hardly a sensible option either, because the chip

down to the pin would require the delicacy of touch of a Seve Ballesteros. All considered, the 7th is what one might call an all-or-nothing hole.

What some may regard as gimmicks should not be permitted to detract from the merits of the course, however, and the US Golf Association underlined that when it awarded the 1989 US Women's Mid-Amateur Championship to Hills of Lakeway. But while

waterfalls are not a Nicklaus speciality, this sort of detail is symptomatic of Nicklaus's meticulousness, which is generally evident and invariably expensive. Nicklaus defends himself as robustly as might be expected. 'I think that those designers who have been good players have an added advantage. Certainly, my golf has helped me with my design concepts.' Hills of Lakeway is an exclusive operation, being open only to club members or students at the connected Academy of Golf. The whole concept is a typically lavish Nicklaus production, but then it is true to say that the only corners cut on one of Jack's courses are on a few of the dog-legs.

18th at Inverness

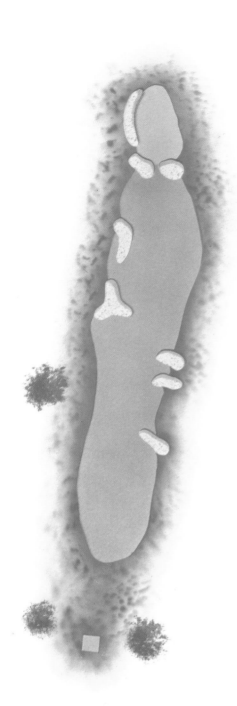

354 YARDS, PAR-4

*A*T 354 YARDS, the final hole at the Inverness Club in Toledo, Ohio, is tailor-made to provide a tournament with a thrilling finale. It begs to be birdied, although no less a man than Jack Nicklaus has remarked: 'It's the hardest easy hole I've ever played.' And it's been responsible for a tremendous climax in three major championships.

The 1931 US Open was as much about stamina as skill. George von Elm holed from 12 feet on the last green to tie with Billy Burke after 72 holes. Playoffs were over 36 holes in those days, and at the first attempt both men shot 149. At the second time of asking Burke prevailed by a stroke, being able to afford three putts on the final green. At the 1957 US Open, both Dick Mayer and Cary Middlecoff made birdie threes on the

18th and another playoff was necessary. Mayer took it easily. But few incidents in golf will be remembered for as long as the manner in which Bob Tway won the 1986 US PGA Championship. He and Greg Norman, the best golfer in the world that year, were level with one hole to play. Tway's approach shot from heavy rough found the right-hand greenside bunker; Norman's ended in a collar of rough just short of the green. Then

Tway, to his ecstatic amazement and Norman's intense mortification, holed out from the trap for a startling birdie that the hapless Australian could not match.

So while it is basically a straightforward drive and a pitch par-4, although not as short as it looks through this telephoto lens, the 18th at Inverness has a rich heritage of drama. The clubhouse, in the background, has a place in golfing history, too. Inver-

ness's first US Open, in 1920, was also the first occasion that professionals had been allowed into the clubhouse at a national championship in either Britain or the United States.

1st at Kennemer (B Course)

ANY IDEA THAT HOLLAND is a wholly flat land is soon dispelled by the first sight of the glorious links of Kennemer, half an hour's drive from Amsterdam and about half a minute's drive from the Grand Prix race track at Zandvoort. The opening hole is typical of what lies ahead. At Kennemer, first impressions are not misleading.

This view from behind the green shows the thatched white clubhouse atop the hillside just behind the first tee. The drive is played downhill – always the most pleasant and satisfying way to begin a round – into a reasonably generous fairway flanked on one side by the omnipresent pine-clad dunes and on the other by some traditionally ferocious links rough. A pair of bunkers in the landing area on either edge of the

fairway await the errant tee shot, and one at each corner of the entrance to the green do the same job in respect of the approach. The character of Kennemer was previously disfigured by wartime fortifications, which spread like an ugly stain across the work of Harry Colt, one of the great pre-war course architects. They were removed in 1947 and now Kennemer is again covered by grass rather than concrete.

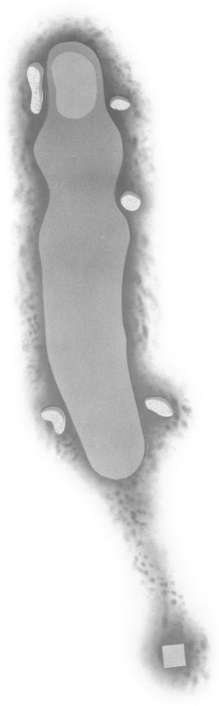

456 YARDS, PAR-4

It is perhaps appropriate to depict Kennemer's first hole here. The course was the scene of the first European tour victory for Spain's Severiano Ballesteros, certainly the best golfer ever produced by the continent of Europe and one of the finest of all post-war golfers. There is also another, more contentious, first involved when discussing golf in the Netherlands. Recent historical research tends to suggest that a rudimentary form of a game which could be classified as golf was played in Holland before it was played in Scotland. That's not a philosophy to be repeated too loudly in St Andrews, but it could be that the first holes on Dutch golf courses were the first holes of all.

12th at La Paz

208 YARDS, PAR-3

O F ALL THE CONTINENTS of the world, the least well endowed with good golf courses – assuming one discounts Antarctica – is South America. The La Paz Country Club, just outside the Bolivian capital, may not be the most venerable of those that are to be found south of Panama but it deserves acclaim not only for being a fine course but for representing the lengths to which some members of the human race will go in order to pursue their favourite pastime. La Paz demonstrates man's ingenuity to man.

The prospect from the 12th tee accords more with one's perception of what golf would look like on the moon rather than on this planet, and in one respect that is not surprising. Golf at La Paz is as near to golf on the moon as man is ever likely to get to on

earth, at least if he wants to stay on grass rather than, as has been done in Peru and Tibet, bat the ball along fairways of rock and putt on greens of mud and tar. The course is 10,886 feet up in the Andes, which is pretty high by any standards but is actually lower than the club used to be until the members resigned themselves to the fact that they were unable to master the agronomical problems posed by trying to keep grass on

their course a further 1500 feet up towards the heavens.

The rarefied air has an obvious impact on the environment. The jagged rocks and petrified flora create a desolate landscape into which it is clearly inadvisable to foozle one's tee shot. Of course, at this altitude club selection can pose problems. The ball flies further through the air; on the other hand, it also falls to the ground more quickly

because of the diminished effect of gravity. But even without the gimmicks of nature, the 12th hole at La Paz would be a genuinely excellent par-3, with trees and sand in close attendance to safeguard its integrity. To walk off the green with a three here is to feel on top of the world.

13th at Medinah (No. 3 Course)

219 YARDS, PAR-3

ALTHOUGH MEDINAH is situated in a suburb of Chicago in the American midwest, both its name and its Byzantine-inspired clubhouse testify to its eastern roots. It was founded by an Arabic order known colloquially as the Shriners, and the influence of the Middle East is also to be found in the name given to the chief landmark of the No.

3 course – Lake Kadijah, so called in honour of Mohammed's wife.

It is the main arm of Lake Kadijah that confronts the golfer as he prepares to play this daunting par-3. Its marshy waters announce a terrifying warning for the player who's afraid of being short, and while not too many club golfers will be in danger of over-hitting this green from the back plates, the kidney-shaped bunker at the rear is

waiting to ensure that if they do the next shot will be no simple chip.

Medinah is presently readying itself to host the 1990 US Open. It will be the third time it has entertained the competitors in its national championship, but on the two preceding occasions – when, before the course was modified, this was the 17th hole – several contenders walked off this green wishing they could have another go. In 1949

Cary Middlecoff won by a stroke, having parred the 17th while his closest rivals, Clayton Heafner and Sam Snead, bogeyed it. In 1975 John Mahaffey was in the clubhouse with 287. Jack Nicklaus needed two pars to match that total but he overshot the green – with a 4-iron! – took four and was finished. Frank Beard, standing on the tee in an identical position, bunkered his tee shot and also failed to salvage his par. That was

the end for him. Ben Crenshaw could have won outright with two pars, but his 2-iron to the 17th found the water and a double-bogey killed his chances. It was left to the unlikely Lou Graham to par the hole, force a playoff with Mahaffey and go on to lift the trophy.

11th at Merion (East Course)

THIS IS NOT ONLY one of the finest holes in American golf but arguably the most historic. In 1930, Bobby Jones stood on the 11th tee at Merion eight up with eight holes to play against his opponent, Eugene Homans, in the final of the US Amateur Championship. Earlier that summer Jones had won the British and US Opens and the British Amateur, and when he secured his par here to close out Homans he completed the 'Impregnable Quadrilateral', the Grand Slam. It remains, and surely will forever, the most remarkable achievement in golf.

That was followed 20 years later by another heroic effort. Ben Hogan conquered two sets of opponents to claim his second US Open – Lloyd Mangrum and George Fazio in a playoff, and the pain and fatigue in his legs which were a legacy of his near-fatal car crash a little over a year before. That was the second of Merion's four US Opens, but although the course measures a mere 6500 yards and is crammed into 126 acres – about half the land occupied by thousands of lesser layouts – it is no push-over for the pros. In the 1971 Open, Jack Nicklaus and Lee Trevino, then the best two golfers in the world, finished with totals of

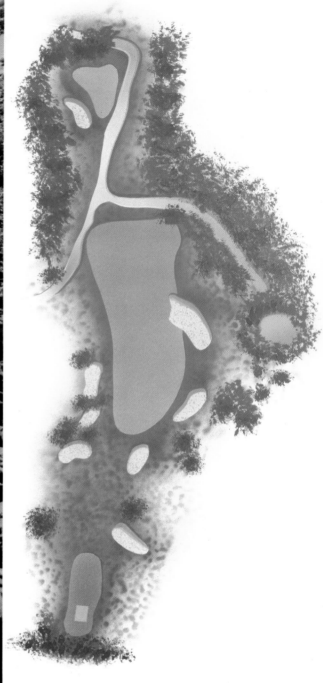

280. That's level par. Trevino took the ensuing playoff after having 90 holes in which to appreciate the ingenuity of Hugh Wilson, who in 1912 turned a pleasant parkland plot in Philadelphia into this tiger-ish golf course. And Merion is not just distinguished, it is distinctive. Instead of flags it has wicker baskets atop the poles on its greens.

Despite being a short par-4, the 11th is one of the strengths of Wilson's design. The driving zone is tight; the green treacherous. It is protected in front, behind and to the right by Cobb's Creek, also known as the Baffling Brook. But the water threatens the drive, too. Gene Sarazen hooked his tee shot into the creek while leading the 1934 US Open. That cost him a seven and he lost the title by a stroke to Olin Dutra.

16th at Morfontaine

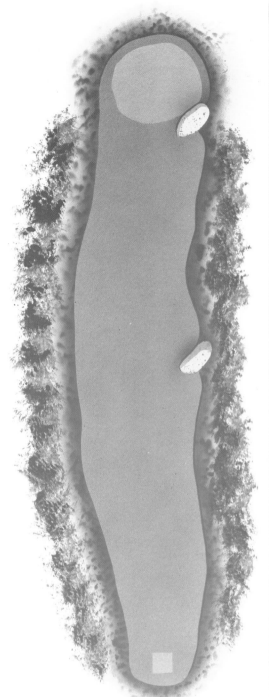

479 YARDS, PAR-4

*T*HE CHIEF REASON that Morfontaine is not better known is that the club wants to keep things that way, and apart from the members' reluctance to have their course opened up to scrutiny and scoring by the game's top professionals, it is generally acknowledged that Morfontaine is too short to test the best. At a little over 6700 yards,

length is not its strength, but this hole is an exception: a par-4 with the yardage of a short par-5, and all the while climbing gradually uphill to a green perched atop a knoll in the forest.

Despite its lack of professional tournament play, Morfontaine has hosted several important amateur events. One such occasion was the 1937 French Championship. The 36-hole final was contested by a French-

man, Jacques Léglise, and an Englishman, that wonderful golf writer, Henry Longhurst. Longhurst was two down with four holes to play, but he won the 15th and then squared the match here, on the 16th, with a solid four. As they left this green, both men remembered Léglise's remark of the morning round when he had been four up playing the short 17th before shanking his tee shot. 'My God', he had said then, 'I shouldn't like

to have to play that shot if we were all-square here this afternoon.' And now they were, but Léglise resolutely found the green at the 17th after Longhurst had done so and went on to win the match. Longhurst noted, 'anyone who knows the psychology of golf will appreciate just how brave a shot it was'.

Longhurst regarded Morfontaine 'as the most attractive course in France'. It, like Chantilly just 10 miles away, was designed

by Tom Simpson, an unorthodox individual who insisted that Longhurst write his obituary before he died. He liked it so much that he ordered 50 copies. But the close relationship between the two men in no way invalidates Longhurst's judgment. The course is elegant to look at yet resistant to scoring, and each hole, like the club, is secluded yet seductive. Morfontaine is one of the secret, unsung treasures of Paris.

15th at Mowbray

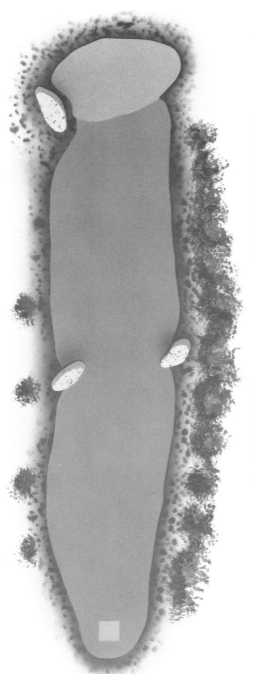

435 YARDS, PAR-4

Golf in South Africa is, like all sporting matters involving that republic, a controversial subject. It can also be an exhilarating experience, and the Mowbray club in Cape Town is one of the most rewarding places in the country at which to enjoy the experience. This hole, the 15th, is one of the most famous in South Africa.

A well-executed tee shot will see one's ball soar into the air and be thrown into sharp relief against the rugged backdrop of Devil's Peak mountain, which dominates the scene. The green can be an elusive target to find with a long iron, for anything which lands short is liable to be thrown off left or right by the undulating fairway. Mowbray has hosted the South African Open on seven occasions, most recently in 1987 when Mark

McNulty was triumphant. McNulty, a Zimbabwean, is just one of the golfers from southern Africa who are presently ranked among the best in the world. One of his predecessors as South African Open champion at Mowbray was the greatest South African golfer in history, Gary Player.

When Player won his country's national Open for the ninth time (of 13 to date) in 1975, the foundations for his victory were laid on the opening day when he fired a 68, four under par, in spite of the notorious south-easter blowing so powerfully that the luxury liner QE2 was unable to berth in Table Bay. Gary is rather given to hyperbole, so it was no surprise to hear him call it 'the best round of my career'. This time he added 'better than my 59 in last year's Brazilian Open'. Player birdied the 15th twice that week, but then he is a marvellous competitor. And then Mowbray encourages that sort of talent, as does the climate – South Africa has a generous ration of 220 days annual sunshine. While Cape Town may not get quite that much, it gets enough to make golf at Mowbray a perennially enjoyable pastime – though if that wind blows hard off the bay, holes such as the 15th will always only be mastered by the likes of Gary Player.

18th at Muirfield

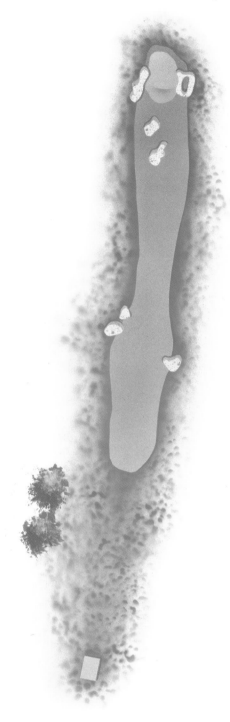

448 YARDS, PAR-4

EYOND THE 18TH GREEN of one of the most demanding finishing holes in championship golf stands the clubhouse of the Honourable Company of Edinburgh Golfers, which is recognized as being the oldest golf club in the world. Nobody can say for sure exactly when it was founded, but it has maintained continuous records since 1744.

Muirfield has not always been its home, however. First it was Leith and then, until 1891, Musselburgh. In 1892 it was the turn of the Honourable Company to put on the Open Championship, so its new course, at Muirfield, near Gullane on the Firth of Forth, received an early baptism at the hands of the best golfers of the age. It also received some harsh criticism. One Scottish professional, Andrew Kirkaldy, called it 'an auld

water meadie', but today it is regarded as the fairest links on the Open roster. It presents its hazards frankly and proudly.

There have been 13 Opens at Muirfield, and fittingly the destiny of the championship has often hinged upon events at the 18th on the final afternoon. A young Gary Player appeared to have squandered the title in 1958 when he drove into a fairway bunker and eventually took a six. To his gratified surprise, his pursuers then faltered, too, and he had won his first major championship. In Muirfield's most recent Open, in 1987, Nick Faldo's concluding drive fell perfectly between the fairway bunkers. A 5-iron and two putts later he had his par (his eighteenth of the round), and soon afterwards he became Open champion when Paul Azinger's approach found the left-hand greenside bunker. It was respect for the bunkers short of the green that caused Harry Vardon to play safe and settle for a five in the 1896 Open. The next day he won the championship for the first of a record six times in a playoff with J.H. Taylor. But the 18th is playable. In 1972 Lee Trevino hit an 8-iron to eight feet to retain the trophy after having chipped in to save his par on the previous hole and thereby destroy Tony Jacklin's morale and, ultimately, his hopes.

17th at Muirfield Village

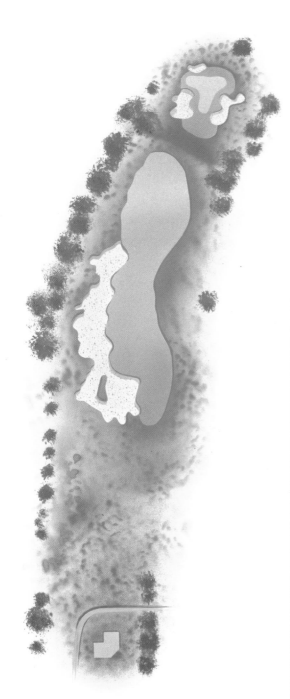

430 YARDS, PAR-4

*T*HE COURSE THAT JACK BUILT, the course where Jack wept. Muirfield Village is Jack Nicklaus's gift to the area where he grew up, near Columbus in Ohio. It is also destined to be remembered in golfing lore as the place where the United States first lost the Ryder Cup on home soil. The American captain on that historic date – 27 September 1987 –

was, of course, also the designer of Muirfield Village, Jack Nicklaus. One might say that he was the architect of his own downfall.

This hole, the 17th, played no small part in the Europeans' victory. The idea from the tee is to put the ball into the left half of the fairway, thus opening up the whole green for the approach shot, but all the while being careful to avoid the gigantic bunker that hugs the left side of the fairway for 50 yards

in the landing area. (When Nicklaus himself won the Memorial Tournament here in 1984, his drive in the final round went the other way: out-of-bounds in a garden to the right. But he saved a bogey five with his second ball and he won the tournament when Andy Bean missed a short putt on this green, then the third hole of a sudden-death playoff.) The competitors in the Ryder Cup generally managed to find the fairway off the tee but

many of the home team were crucially undone by either the greenside traps or the grassy valley in front of the green.

The tone for the entire contest was set on the opening morning. Larry Mize and Lanny Wadkins went into the thick stuff and lost their nerve and soon afterwards their match against Nick Faldo and Ian Woosnam. They had been four up after nine holes. That afternoon Andy Bean (not a happy hole for

him) and Mark Calcavecchia both bogeyed the hole and thereby lost it to a par – an almost unpardonable sin in fourballs – in their battle with Bernhard Langer and Sandy Lyle. When they did exactly the same thing at the last hole the writing was clearly on the wall for the hosts. It was therefore fitting that when Seve Ballesteros tapped in the winning putt for Europe on that fateful Sunday, it should be on the 17th green that he did it.

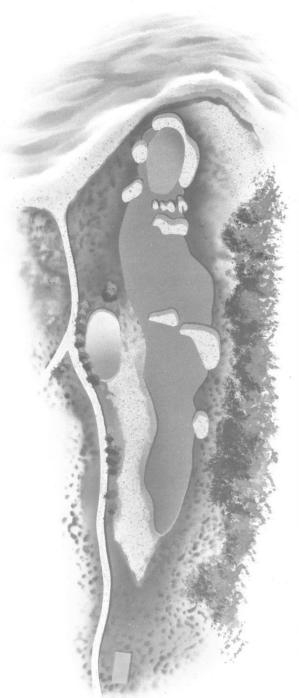

375 YARDS, PAR-4

ALTHOUGH THE NATIONAL Golf Links of America is ill-named in one respect – its turf is of an inland character rather than of the sandy substance upon which a genuine links is built – it is entirely appropriate that it should take a name which so unabashedly pays homage to its British heritage. Its creator, Charles Blair Macdonald, who in 1895 won the first US Amateur Championship, drew inspiration for his design primarily from the great links courses of the British Isles. The 17th hole is not one of the more obvious transatlantic transplants (elsewhere there are virtually carbon copies of celebrated holes at St Andrews, Royal St George's, Prestwick and North Berwick) but it assuredly contains the elements of British golf that Macdonald admired.

The full nature of the hole is captured from the tee. Even the scorecard bears a hint of Scotland, with each hole having a name in the traditional fashion. The 17th is called 'Peconic', on account of the stretch of water at which the drive is aimed – Peconic Bay, towards the far eastern end of Long Island, New York. Clearing the sandy scrub with the tee shot should not pose too many difficulties for the reasonably adept golfer,

but the cross-bunkers catch many a faint-hearted drive which attempts to minimize the carry across the waste. Thereafter, the approach shot has to be bold enough to sail over the sand in front of the green yet be sufficiently well judged to stop short of the semi-circular trap that runs round the whole of its back part.

The National was not the first course in the United States (it is 18 years younger

than its neighbour at Shinnecock Hills) but it was the most influential pre-war layout. Macdonald's aim was to construct 18 holes without a weak point among them, under-pinned by his philosophy of forcing the player to make a choice with every shot: essentially, whether to play safe or to be rewarded (or penalized) for taking the heroic route. On the 17th, as on the other holes, Macdonald succeeded in his goal.

14th at New St Andrews

160 YARDS, PAR-3

T HE JAPANESE ARE the most aggressive exporters in the world when it comes to business. In golf, they are the most voracious importers. They have unashamedly brought a name halfway around the world to bestow upon this golf course close to Tokyo, their country's capital city. They have not actually copied the holes of the Old Course at St

Andrews in Scotland – which one might justifiably describe as golf's capital city – but they have taken the name. Even the scorecards are printed with a tartan cover.

In Japan, the people who are members of clubs like New St Andrews are prepared to pay fees on the exorbitant side of excessive in order to become one of the few who have a golf course to play on rather than be one of the millions who are consigned to an eternity

on a driving range. Getting the opportunity to step onto the fairways of a real golf course is a genuine and rare treat for most Japanese, which is perhaps the main reason why it's often six hours before they come off it.

The 14th at New St Andrews can certainly detain one a little while. The stone wall in the foreground forms an attractive backdrop to a shot played from an upraised tee, usually with something like a 7-iron. But the green is not of a particularly generous size, and if the ball catches the wrong slope on the contoured surface it may well be thrown into one of the hole's four encircling bunkers. It is not for nothing that the 14th is widely regarded as the best of the New Course's quartet of short holes, and if the wind is up, the target from the tee can appear to be intimidatingly small. If the memory of a disaster here proves so bad that sleep becomes impossible, then at this club there is always the chance to conquer the recollections of a golfing nightmare with a game at night. New St Andrews is equipped with floodlights. In the land of the rising sun, it could be said – only half in jest – that the sun never sets on New St Andrews.

16th at Oakland Hills (South Course)

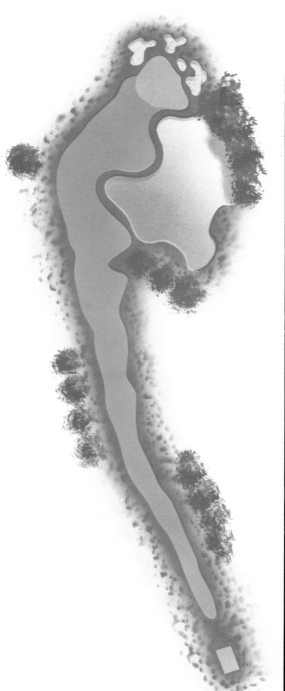

405 YARDS, PAR-4

W HEN DONALD ROSS, the expatriate Scotsman who built so many of the best courses in the United States, first set eyes upon the property which now belongs to the Oakland Hills Country Club in Birmingham, Michigan, he remarked: 'The Lord intended this for a golf course.' On the other hand, this is also the place dubbed the 'monster'

by the great Ben Hogan – and that was after he had won the third of his four US Open titles here in 1951 with a closing 67, one of just two scores below the par of 70 all week and one of the greatest rounds in history.

Hogan's caustic comment was in response to the modifications ordered by Robert Trent Jones when, just as he was to be employed to do at Baltusrol, he was hired by the club to tighten up the course

before that Open of 1951. He achieved his objective primarily by introducing over 50 new bunkers, mostly in the landing area for a good drive, and deepening the greenside traps. This view from behind the green of the dog-leg 16th suggests precisely why Oakland Hills has acquired an awesome reputation for toughness. The pond is patently not the only hazard.

Nevertheless, the 16th is playable. In the 1985 US Open, the eventual winner, Andy North, sank a putt of 60 feet on this green for his only birdie of the third round. By the next evening he had captured the championship for a second time with a stroke to spare. Thirteen years previously, Gary Player was tied for the lead on the final afternoon of the US PGA Championship when he sliced his drive into the rough behind the weeping willows on the left of the picture. He felt he needed a 7-iron to reach the green but he had to hit a 9-iron in order to be able to get his ball over the trees. Pumped up with adrenalin, Player swung hard, his ball cleared the willows and the water and settled down four feet from the cup. He had turned a bogey into a birdie and, having saved par from seven feet at the daunting par-3 17th (in the right background), he went on to win by two shots.

3rd at Oakmont

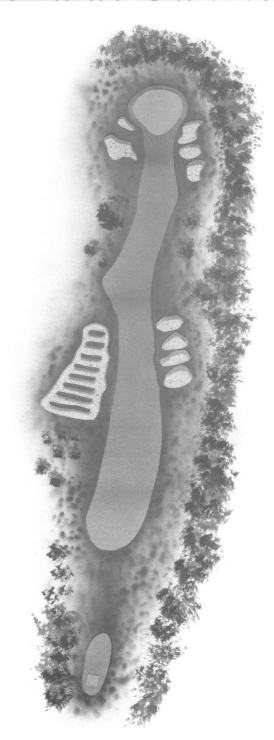

N 1987 OAKMONT WAS accorded the honour of being the first golf course in the United States to be designated a national historic landmark. It is perhaps just as well that didn't happen shortly after the course was opened in 1904 when it had eight par-5s, one par-6 and 220 bunkers. Things have been toned down a bit since then, but

Oakmont is located just outside Pittsburgh, Pennsylvania – otherwise known as Steeltown, USA – and to get round it one has to be as hard as nails, or as hard as Oakmont's notoriously fast greens, on which putting has been compared to trying to stop the ball halfway down a marble staircase. During the 1935 US Open, the eventual runner-up, Jimmy Thomson, claimed that the dime he had used to mark his ball on one hole had

slid right off the slick, treacherous green.

Oakmont is still proud of possessing greens of almost illegal speed, and the bunkers that remain are both sufficiently plentiful and punishing to cause great anguish, even though the club has long abandoned its former sadistic practice of using a furrowed rake to comb the sand.

The most infamous of Oakmont's hazards is this bunker, known as the Church Pews on account of the serried grass ridges that occupy it. This view is of the 3rd hole, where the elevated green means that the approach shot will play longer than the card suggests, but the Church Pews are positioned to trap a hooked or pulled drive on the 4th as well. Johnny Miller birdied both holes on the final day of the 1973 US Open, which he went on to win with an eight-under-par 63. Like Hogan's at Oakland Hills, it remains one of the greatest rounds in history. In the most recent of Oakmont's six US Opens, in 1983, Larry Nelson visited the Church Pews on the 3rd in the third round, took the almost inevitable bogey and dropped to seven over par for the championship. But Nelson is a devout man, and maybe his prayers were answered in there. He covered the next 33 holes in 11 under par to beat Tom Watson by a stroke.

4th at Oak Tree

IF THINGS HAD TURNED out differently, this hole could have been immortalized as the setting for one of the more remarkable moments in major championship history. Standing on this tee, Paul Azinger held the lead in the third round of the 1988 US PGA Championship at Oak Tree in Edmond, Oklahoma. After he had played the 4th, his

grip on the title seemed to have tightened.

Azinger selected a 6-iron to make the carry over the water, which terrifies the lesser players on this hole as it does on many others at Oak Tree. The flag was set towards the front-right corner of the green, meaning that Azinger did not have much margin for error if he wanted to get his ball close to the stick. On the other hand, he did not want to choose a club which would put

him over the back of the green facing a chip back down over a ridge towards the lake. Azinger's choice was perfect. His tee shot landed on line some 15 feet below the hole and rolled on in. It could have become one of the most celebrated holes-in-one in history. That it probably won't is down to the fact that Azinger followed his ace by taking a double-bogey seven at the 5th – some consolation for the handicap golfer who

almost traditionally makes a mess of a hole when his judgment is clouded by the euphoria of a success at the previous one – and just over 24 hours later he had finished runner-up, three shots behind fellow-American Jeff Sluman.

Azinger's shot was made to seem less than miraculous not only by his ultimate failure to win but by the fact that there were three other holes-in-one at Oak Tree that week. Often, holing out with an iron shot seems to be the only way to survive this Pete Dye design, which was relatively gentle to the PGA competitors only because of the absence of its customary strong winds off the Oklahoma plains. Oak Tree is, according to the US Golf Association, the toughest par-71 course in the nation. Azinger found the ideal way to conquer one of its toughest holes, but in the end Oak Tree conquered him.

18th at Olympic (Lake Course)

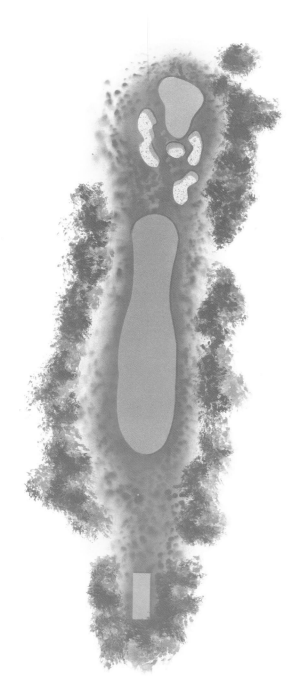

343 YARDS, PAR-4

THE OLYMPIC CLUB in San Francisco has staged three US Opens since the Second World War but one could forgive its members if they seriously question whether it has been worth their while to have relinquished their course for the purpose of hosting their country's national title.

Olympic is the place where heroes have

been humiliated by hobos. In 1955, unknown Jack Fleck denied Ben Hogan a record fifth title; in 1966, the colourless Billy Casper made up seven shots over the final nine holes to catch the charismatic Arnold Palmer and then beat him in a playoff; and in 1987, Scott Simpson was the unlikely God-fearing, church-going villain who vanquished the popular Tom Watson.

The 18th played an especially vital role

in the first of those three upsets. Hogan was reckoned to be home and dry in the final round – indeed, television had gone off the air having announced that he was the winner, and Hogan himself had informally proffered his ball to the USGA for display in its museum as the one which had clinched that eternally elusive fifth US Open – until Fleck birdied the short 15th and then fired his approach to within seven feet of the pin at the last and sank the putt for a tying birdie. Fleck was given no chance of taking the playoff, but as they arrived on the 18th tee he led Hogan by a stroke. Hogan had the honour, but his left foot slipped while he was on the downswing and his ball hurtled into impossible rough on the left. It was quite an achievement to reach the green in five and hole out for a six, but Fleck had his par and the greatest prize of his life. This photograph gives an idea of the view facing Hogan as he prepared to hit that final drive. Scores of eucalyptus, pine and cypress trees line the fairway, and even after a straight tee shot (with either a wood or a long iron) there is a demanding pitch to be played. The green, which hugs the hillside beneath the clubhouse, is endowed with a wickedly canted putting surface and surrounded by a battery of deep bunkers.

13th at Paraparaumu Beach

THERE ARE NOT MANY tremendous links courses anywhere in the world outside the British Isles, and most of the rest are in Europe. This is therefore a distinguished exception. Some 30 miles from Wellington, on New Zealand's North Island, Paraparaumu Beach overlooks the Tasman Sea and is at the same time overlooked itself by the

mountains of the hinterland. Peter Thomson has called it the only true championship links in either New Zealand or Australia, and as a five-time winner of the British Open he should know. The only left-hander to win that championship, indeed the only 'leftie' to win any major championship, was Bob Charles, who won the Open at Royal Lytham in 1963 and who once had a tournament round of 62 at Paraparaumu Beach.

The 13th may be the pick of the holes at Paraparaumu. Whether played by handicap golfers, or by tour professionals when the club takes its turn to host prestigious events such as the New Zealand Open, it embodies all the elements that appeal to the lover of links golf – tumbling fairways of firm, sand-based turf dashed in colours of green and brown; the unpredictability of the bounce of the ball as it meets the ridges and undula-

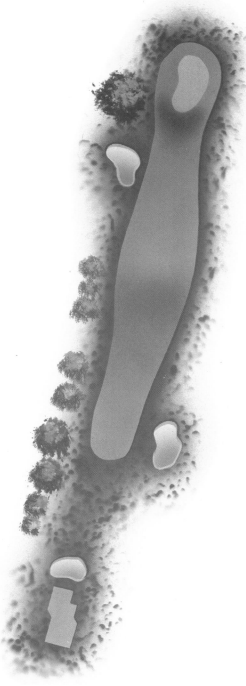

454 YARDS, PAR-4

tions of the fairway; and a wind off the ocean. One singular aspect of Paraparaumu is that for a links it has very few sand bunkers, but on the 13th, as on another great links hole featured in this book, the 11th at Ballybunion, the omission is hardly a blemish.

As it is, the 13th at Paraparaumu is a severe test anyway. The drive has to be long and straight in order to offer a decent sight of the green and to give a decent chance of reaching it in two blows across the profusion of humps and hollows. To mis-hit is to fall prey to the vagaries of the bounce; to mis-hit woefully is to court a lost ball and a shot lost in the little pond to the left.

7th at Pebble Beach

ROBERT LOUIS STEVENSON called the coastline of Carmel Bay 'the finest meeting of land and sea in the world'. Thousands of people who have been fortunate enough to take in the view of the Pacific shoreline adjoining Pebble Beach Golf Links in California have been willing to echo Stevenson's assessment, and the 7th tee at Pebble Beach is as good a place as any from which to marvel at the wonders of nature and to reflect on the occasional wisdom of man in making the best use of that which God has put at his disposal.

This is the shortest hole in championship golf, but in the two US Opens held at Pebble Beach the 7th has been the scene of high drama on the final afternoon. In 1972 Jack Nicklaus, one of the most powerful golfers the game has seen, had to punch as much as a 7-iron into the right-to-left wind coming in off the ocean, which made the tiny green seem even smaller and the perils of sand and sea even sterner. But Nicklaus found his target and holed for a birdie. That settled him down after an indifferent opening and he went on to win by three shots. Ten years later Nicklaus came to the 7th having birdied the preceding four holes. He

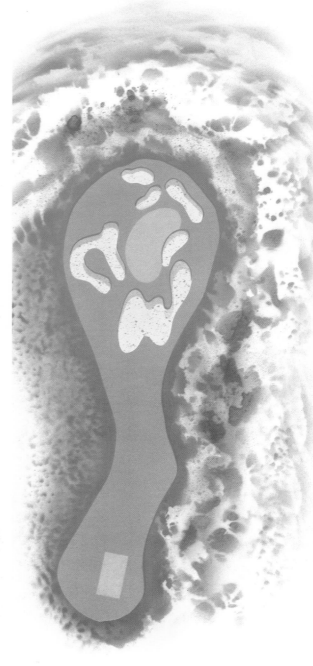

only needed a sand wedge this time. He knocked his ball to 11 feet and sank it to move to five under par – in the lead and on course for a record fifth US Open. Shortly afterwards, Tom Watson played an even better tee shot but missed a birdie chance from two feet. Tournaments can often hinge upon such things, but not this time. Watson stormed home in 32 and wrapped matters up by chipping in, almost miraculously, for a birdie two on the penultimate hole.

In the opinion of many experts, Pebble is one of the best golf courses in the world. It has certainly been one of the best known since 1958, when the famous Bing Crosby Pro-Am started to be televised across America, and it is unique in being the only public course to have staged the US Open.

17th at PGA West (TPC Stadium Course)

F CONTEMPORANEITY and controversy in golf course architecture appeal to you in approximately equal measure, then this course at PGA West is what you are looking for. The players on the US PGA Tour loved it so much that they got it kicked off the rota for the Bob Hope Classic. 'Spiteful, hateful', Ray Floyd called it. Tom Watson weighed in with 'Awful, artificial, unfair and ugly'. A third former winner of the US Open, Lee Trevino, volunteered: 'I know some courses which are easier than the practice ground here.' That was before he holed his tee shot on this hole, the 17th, to win $175,000 for that single stroke in the 1987 Skins Game. Other choice comments include 'PGA West looks like downtown Beirut' and 'Sending an amateur onto this course is like sending Little Red Riding Hood into the Casbah'. Veteran pro Leonard Thompson said of the designer, Pete Dye: 'Thank God this guy isn't building airports.'

If you have not yet got the picture, maybe this one will give you the idea. Dye shifted over two million yards of 'dirt' and constructed eight lakes to create PGA West from the rugged country around Palm Springs in the California desert. The 17th is

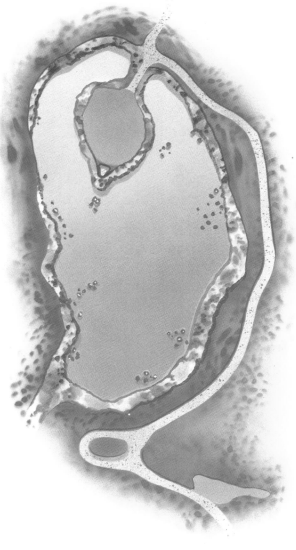

modelled on the equivalent hole at the TPC at Sawgrass in Florida, the original 'stadium golf course', and in addition to being an utterly unforgiving par-3, which offers the 'chicken' no alternative to putting round the cartpath if he feels the green is out of his range, it presents a typical PGA West landscape. The hole is nicknamed 'Alcatraz' – like the old San Francisco prison, it's surrounded by rocks and water. 'There is no escape' is the club's slogan for the 17th. Being in that evil pot bunker cut into the front of the green is almost good news.

The 1991 Ryder Cup will be held at PGA West, although there had been talk of it being moved. Perhaps the hosts were not so much afraid of losing another match on home soil as losing all their balls in home waters.

17th at Pinehurst (No. 2 Course)

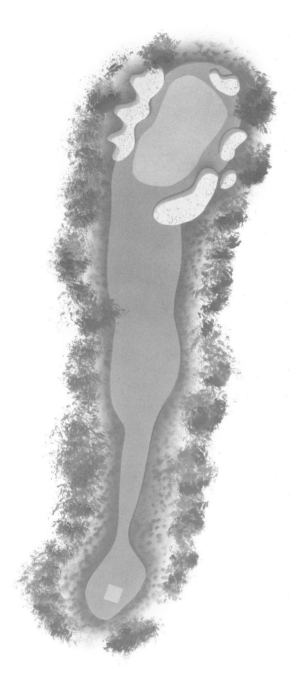

190 YARDS, PAR-3

ONALD ROSS has already made an appearance in these pages as the course architect at Oakland Hills. But this course is generally acknowledged to be his *tour de force*, with the subtle undulations and run-offs around the greens of the No. 2 Course at Pinehurst being reminiscent of the slopes to be found at Dornoch in Scotland, where Ross

grew up and learned the rudiments of his profession before journeying to the United States to establish his reputation.

Pinehurst is located in the flat sandhills of North Carolina. A Boston pharmacist, James Tufts, originally purchased property at Pinehurst because the cost of land at $1 an acre was a small price to pay for a place to build a winter retreat. Later he took to golf and discovered what has long since been

understood – that the worst land for agriculture is the best for golf. The sand-based terrain means that Pinehurst's golfers enjoy the sensation of striking the ball off almost links-like turf, and the rave reviews of those who have played No. 2 since its opening in 1907 have led to it being commonly regarded among both the most stringent and aesthetically satisfying tests in the United States.

The 17th epitomizes the qualities of Pinehurst. The proud pines form a serene, silent audience for the weak-hearted facing a long iron into a well-protected green, creating a rather exaggerated feeling of claustrophobia. Although there will always be other golfers on the course at Pinehurst, each hole is cut through the firs, thereby suggesting a splendid isolation. It is a fitting mood at Pinehurst because, although it has hosted the US PGA Championship and the Ryder Cup once each, it is because of its relative remoteness and the fact that until 1987 it had bermuda rather than bent-grass greens that Pinehurst has so far been denied the privilege of staging the US Open. Now only the remoteness remains as an obstacle.

18th at Pine Valley

OF ALL THE GREAT COURSES in this book, Pine Valley above all can truly claim to be able to put up any one of its holes as a credible candidate for inclusion here. Pine Valley is the almost whimsical creation of George Crump, a millionaire Philadelphia hotelier who supervised the beginnings of his one and only golf course project in the New Jersey sandhills in 1913 but sadly had to leave its completion to Harry Colt and Hugh Wilson following his death in 1918.

Pine Valley is not only whimsical but winsome – that is, it is usually the course that is left with the winning smile. Pine Valley's glorious evergreens make it a beautiful place, but the course is dressed to kill. The 18th has its share of agonizing anecdotes; tales of hapless victims tormented and then undone by its caprices. Perhaps the best illustration of the terrible end that can befall a player here is the story of a man who was good enough to stand on this tee, facing this view, needing a par for a 78. Instead he took a one-putt 17 for a 91. On the other hand, Sam Randolph just about secured the Americans' victory in the 1985 Walker Cup when, after skying his tee shot on this hole, he smote a majestic 3-wood to

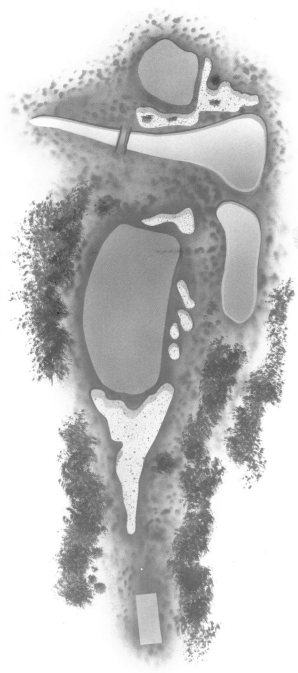

within 20 feet of the hole to save his par and the match.

Pine Valley has been called 'a 184-acre bunker' by one demoralized professional. The 36-hole club championship has been won with a total of 173, 33 over par. Its par-3s have cost good golfers scores in the 30s and 40s. Hit the ball into its dark forests or Sahara-like wastelands and it is probably gone forever. People have even lost their playing partners here. Club traditionalists sadistically insist that even in its most penal hazards, the ball must be played from where it is – a drop under penalty for an unplayable lie is not permitted. And yet its fairways are generous, as this picture shows. Pine Valley is fair but fearsome, and the pleasures of success are enhanced by knowing the price of failure.

15th at Portmarnock

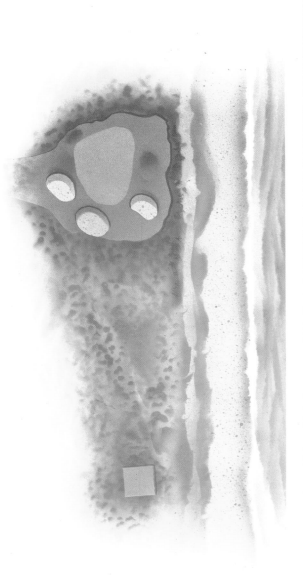

188 YARDS, PAR-3

Some days, the Royal & Ancient Golf Club of St Andrews must wish that things were different. Portmarnock would be an ideal venue for the Open Championship. It is a great links course, with space for all the extra amenities that the modern Open demands, and it is just outside a capital city in the British Isles. The problem is that the capital is Dublin and that Portmarnock is in the Irish Republic, not in England, Scotland or Wales. As a result, the club has to settle for hosting what is perhaps the second most prestigious golf championship in the British Isles – the Irish Open, where the crowds are vast and enthusiastic and where the players have to contend with a course that separates the men from the boys.

The winner of the 1988 Irish Open was a

little chap who, at 5 ft 4½ in, is the height of a boy but with a game which is very much the envy of his fellow men. Ian Woosnam succeeded two other top European golfers, Severiano Ballesteros and Bernhard Langer, as winner of the title at Portmarnock, and this hole may have witnessed the turning point in his triumph. It is apparent that to stray too far to the right off the tee, either in attempting to draw the ball into the pin with the help of the wind off the sea or in losing control of a fade which has started left of the target, is to be out-of-bounds on the beach. That is the fate that befell Woosnam in the second round but, in playing three from the tee, his next shot managed to cling onto the putting surface, some 40 feet from the hole. When that putt rolled in, Woosnam had saved a bogey four from what could easily have been a six, and he eventually romped home from the field by seven shots.

If the wind were not a sufficient hazard on this hole, the 15th green is protected in front by three typically tyrannical bunkers – another hallmark of a great links. And the R & A appreciate it. Although they cannot take the Open Championship to Portmarnock, they have selected it to host the 1991 Walker Cup when that is contested in Ireland for the first time.

3rd at Princeville (Ocean Course)

*L*UXURIANT FOLIAGE is in abundant supply on the Princeville course, a Pacific paradise on the Hawaiian island of Kauai. Hot sun and regular rainfall combine to nourish this ancient volcanic landscape. Beyond the green on the 3rd hole of the Ocean nine at Princeville (the resort possesses 27 holes altogether) lies a veritable jungle. Exotic

trees adorn the fairways and the rough, and instead of using white posts to indicate to the golfer that he is 150 yards from the green, the club has planted hyacinths.

It was against this backdrop that *South Pacific* was filmed, and in real life the aspect from the 3rd tee at Princeville – condominiums excepted – looks every bit as enchanting as it does on the silver screen. But there is no need for 150-yard markers, however

attractively constructed, on this hole. Its length is noted on the card, and its hazards are equally plain to see from the tee some 60 feet above the green. Too short means a splash, too long means in the bush, and nobody but a masochist would relish playing a bunker shot down towards the flag from one of those two traps. And as if the visible difficulties were not sufficiently problematical, not to mention picturesque, the golfer will

invariably be teased by the direction, strength and constancy of the 15-20 mile per hour trade winds as he conducts his own internal, mental debate as to which club to hit from the tee.

Robert Trent Jones Jnr, who designed Princeville, spoke of his fears on surveying the site when he said: 'If there is a finer place to build a golf course, I haven't seen it. On such great terrain in such a beautiful spot, I was scared stiff I might muff it.' He was provided with ample reassurance that he hadn't when Princeville was awarded the 1978 World Cup, an honour which acknowledged that Jones had indeed created a course worthy of its setting. Princeville is a holiday course alright, but it is also rather more than that.

10th at Riviera

THIS IS THE SORT OF HOLE where one will frequently walk onto the tee with a birdie in mind and walk off the green with a bogey on the card. The Riviera club at Pacific Palisades, Los Angeles, has an illustrious pedigree and a course to match, which means that there has to be room for one of the most delightful challenges in golf: the short par-4.

The 10th is the shortest of the fours at Riviera, but a pair of greedy fairway bunkers and a generous supply of sand around the tight, angled green may have something to say to those optimists who stand on the tee and survey the hole's gentle right-hand dog-leg under a balmy, blue Californian sky. There may even be a temptation to try to drive the hole, but failure to reach the target will leave a delicate pitch over a bunker to a

green that slopes sharply away. Driving out to the left is simpler and safer – only an iron from the tee is required – and that opens up the green for a relatively straightforward approach shot.

Being a near neighbour to Hollywood, Riviera is not averse to a little ostentation, as the imposing clubhouse on the hillside might indicate. Not that such an attitude is misplaced. Douglas Fairbanks was perhaps

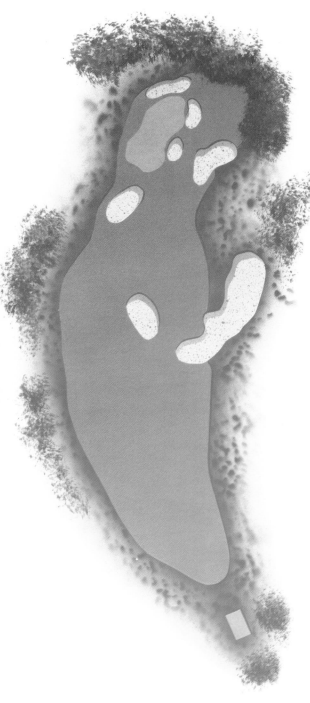

321 YARDS, PAR-4

the first of many film stars to become a member, and much of Ben Hogan's life story – the movie *Follow The Sun* – was shot on location here. Following his near-fatal car crash in February 1949, Hogan made his return to tournament golf at Riviera 11 months later in the Los Angeles Open. Although he found simply walking extremely painful and tiring, he was only beaten after a playoff with Sam Snead. The famous Amer-ican columnist, Red Smith, suggested that Hogan's performance might have been the most remarkable effort in sports history. Two summers previously, Hogan had been at Riviera in happier circumstances, winning the first of his four US Opens. Afterwards he acknowledged that victory had been virtually sealed with the 15-footer he sank for a birdie three at the 10th.

8th at Rose Hall

2 AMAICA'S MONTEGO BAY is one of the most alluring-sounding places in the world. To the east of the celebrated holiday resort lies a course which offers the singular delights of golf in the Caribbean. This picture of the approach shot to the 8th green captures both the beauty of the environment and the difficulty of the task in hand.

The entire left side of this hole runs alongside the beach and the beckoning surf. The aggressive line to the flag means that there is no margin for error, either short, long or left, but nobody wants to go to play golf on holiday with a view to laying up. At least on this occasion the hole has been cut in a relatively friendly spot on the green, but even so there is a substantial reward for taking a braver line from the tee. The closer

one's drive finishes to the shoreline, the more lofted the club with which one can play the second shot.

The 8th at Rose Hall may be the course's most dramatic oceanside hole, but the layout offers plenty of attractions elsewhere and inland. The back nine moves into quite mountainous terrain, and there is a waterfall close to the 15th hole which was used as the setting for a scene from the

James Bond film *Live and Let Die*. It was an appropriate location given that Bond's creator, Ian Fleming, a keen golfer like his fictional secret agent (see Royal St George's), decided on the name for his 'hero' while staying on Jamaica. James Bond was the name of the author of a book on ornithology which rested on Fleming's shelves. Fleming liked the name, used it and made it famous throughout the world. Rose Hall's reputation does not extend that far, though the course has some folklore of its own. Stories abound of the White Witch of Rose Hall, Annee Palmer, who in the last century allegedly murdered three husbands at her home near to where the course now runs, but these days the talk around the club is more about Arnie Palmer.

12th at Royal Birkdale

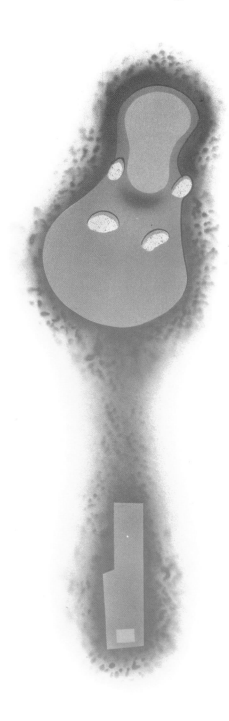

190 YARDS, PAR-3

THE HOLE WHICH TOM WATSON considers the best at Royal Birkdale, and indeed one of the greatest short holes in the world, has only been in existence for some 25 years. The majestic Southport links had already held two Open Championships before Fred Hawtree was brought in to update the course. Earlier modifications had been undertaken by his father, who had intended to include this hole in his design until financial constraints dictated otherwise. When the Open returned to Birkdale in 1965, the new 12th proved itself with a vengeance. On the final round both Peter Thomson, the eventual champion, and his playing partner, Tony Lema, were deceived by the contours of the green into missing putts from inside a yard.

Perhaps more than any other hole at Royal Birkdale, which is renowned for its hugely imposing sandhills, the 12th illustrates why the links has been described as the first stadium golf course built by God. Pete Dye's work at PGA West and at the TPC in Florida has nothing on this. Royal Birkdale is not only a great examination of golf but also an immensely enjoyable arena for golf watching.

The wild beauty of the 12th is a tribute to Hawtree's ability to make the optimum use of the terrain. The green looks to be so naturally sited that the Lord Himself might have cut it into the dunes, though one could forgive Nick Faldo if he felt less than ecstatic about the hole at the 1983 Open. He was tied for the lead in the closing stages until he missed the green here and took four. He had to wait four years until he

realized his most cherished ambition by winning the Open for the first time. Tom Watson only had to wait another couple of hours to realize an ambition of his by winning the Open for the first time in England – and for the fifth time altogether. But his complimentary remark about the 12th was delivered at the start of the week, so it was said with candour rather than cant.

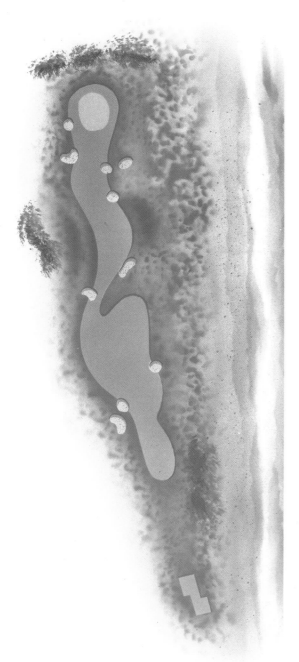

418 YARDS, PAR-4

THE PROSPECT OF TACKLING a tough par-4 is one of the most potentially card-damaging challenges in golf, but there are few places as stimulating as Royal County Down at Newcastle in Northern Ireland in which to face it. Old Tom Morris laid out the links in 1889 at a fee 'not exceeding £4', and in one respect his design was something of a first. Rather than being a standard out-and-back layout in the fashion of most links, County Down has two loops of nine holes, each returning to the clubhouse, which means that the wind assails the golfer from all directions on both nines.

The reputation of a great links is generally based solely upon the greatness of its holes. Seldom does scenery play a signi-ficant role in the acclaim it receives. County

Down is a spectacular exception. The blue sea and golden sand of Dundrum Bay, the majesty of the Mountains of Mourne, dominated by Slieve Donard, the highest peak: these are among the reasons why the much travelled and much respected English golf writer, Peter Dobereiner, is prepared to forgive Newcastle's over-reliance on blind tee shots, and even blind approaches, and declare that there is nowhere else in the world that he would rather play golf.

The 3rd is not among the more secretive holes, and one of the things the golfer sees on arriving on the tee is that the drive must hold the left side of the fairway if he is to grant himself an uninterrupted view of the huge marker post at the back of the green as he surveys his second shot, from a point around the ridge which traverses the fairway, and considers how best to try to reach his target nestling between the dunes and the bunkers. County Down is crammed with marvellous holes like this, and although political, commercial and other considerations will preclude it from ever hosting the Open Championship, it has at least had the honour of staging the Amateur Championship. That was in 1970 when Michael Bonallack completed an unprecedented hat-trick of victories in the event.

THESE DAYS THE EUROPEAN golf circuit is not confined to Europe. This course was voted the best-conditioned venue on the 1987 PGA European Tour. It looks rather like a well-maintained American layout, which is perhaps not too surprising considering that it was designed by an American, the esteemed Robert Trent Jones. In fact, the course is actually in Africa – just outside Rabat in Morocco – and its regal patronage has no connection with the Prince of Wales who was responsible for bestowing the royal prefix upon so many British courses, some of which are included in this book, in the latter years of the 19th century. Royal Dar-es-Salam's Red Course was completed in 1971 at the behest of King Hassan II of Morocco.

As much as the tour professionals re-spected the manner in which it was pre-sented for their pleasure for the Moroccan Open, they also respected the calibre of the course: a par-73 measuring 7362 yards and playing every inch of that over its lush fairways which run like emerald ribbons through relentless rows of cork oaks. Royal Dar-es-Salam is surely the best course on the continent outside South Africa. The 12th embodies all its virtues.

It is long, in keeping with the character of the entire course. It is attractive, and the Greco-style columns in the centre of the photograph, which stand grandly between the 11th and 12th fairways, provide an added, architectural diversion. But one's attention cannot be diverted too seriously or else water, for the fourth consecutive hole, could lead to a classical golfing tragedy. Most players, even the more powerful ones, will opt for prudence on this hole and settle for getting home in three shots rather than two. That is what Howard Clark did in the final round of the inaugural Moroccan Open in March 1987, and he was rewarded with a birdie four which enabled him to catch Mark James, the man he had pushed into second place when the tournament finished six holes later.

5th at Royal Dornoch

361 YARDS, PAR-4

ORNOCH HAS BEEN KNOWN to golfers at least since 1616, which means it stands behind only St Andrews and Leith, in Edinburgh, in terms of having the longest established connection with the game. But for over 350 years it was comparatively ignored, deemed to be, if not beyond the pale, beyond the range of a car's petrol tank. It is over 600 miles north of London, 90 minutes drive north of Inverness. Dornoch is in Sutherland, in the north-eastern tip of Scotland, but lately its remoteness has, almost perversely, served to increase the esteem in which it is held. Today it is frequently cited as the major inspiration to contemporary golf course architects. One of them, Pete Dye, whose work comes under scrutiny several times within these pages, said after

his first visit to the place: 'No other links has quite the ageless aura Dornoch does.'

Its influence goes back further than Dye. Donald Ross was raised on the lessons taught by its intrinsic charms, and he applied his knowledge in the United States at courses such as Pinehurst No. 2. This view of the 5th hole emphasizes the inherent beauty of an unspoilt links, with its crisp turf, grassy mounds and unkempt bunkers. The plateau green, which owes its genesis to nature rather than to man, is also typically Dornoch, invariably rebuffing an indifferent shot.

The drive is played from a tee perched in the hillside to a billowing fairway in the valley below. The second shot then has to clear a barrage of bunkers to reach the haven of the green in the distance. The 6th hole, an excellent par-3, is visible beyond it, hugging the gorse-clad bank and looking for all the world as if it had been nestling there for centuries. Not so. That hole was added after World War II – perforce, because part of the course had been destroyed. But the 5th remains unaltered, a tribute to time and to the abiding genius of nature.

18th at Royal Hong Kong (Composite)

Given that even the Communists have now succumbed to the lure of golf, it is likely that when the British pass control of Hong Kong on to the Chinese in 1997 the future of the Royal Hong Kong Golf Club will be secure. The change in the status of what is currently a Crown Colony will probably not prevent the perpetuation of the ties with a bygone age, as represented by the foundation of the original club by the British in 1889 and the naming of the three courses at its present premises as the Old, the New and the Eden – the three major courses at St Andrews in Scotland, the place revered the world over as 'the Home of Golf'.

When the club hosts the Hong Kong Open each February, the tournament is played over an amalgam of the New and Eden courses. Eastern golfers are always to the fore in the championship, although past winners have included former British Open champions Peter Thomson and Greg Norman (both Australians) and Orville Moody, US Open champion in 1969. In 1987, Welshman Ian Woosnam became the first British winner of the event and he then went on to win seven more times around the world during that year.

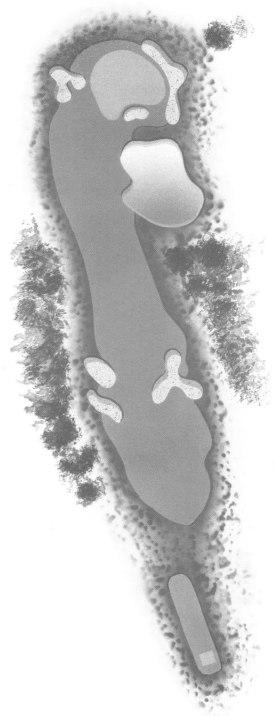

417 YARDS, PAR-4

The 18th hole is a formidable obstacle for those who reach it needing a four to join those illustrious names in the record books. The drive is a tight one, but most players have to go with the driver in order to leave as short a shot as possible into the flag. The lake just in front of the green has swallowed up many mis-hit or misjudged second shots, including that of Japan's Seiichi Kanai in 1983. He required a birdie to catch Norman but finished, via the bunker, with a seven. Three years later he arrived on the 18th tee wanting a par to force a playoff. This time he got home in two and knocked in a putt of 20 feet for a three and the title. But even before that he had surely known it was to be his day. He had already holed-in-one at the 5th.

117

9th at Royal Lytham and St Annes

LYTHAM IS ONE OF just three English courses presently on the rota of hosts to the Open Championship. The Open is only ever played on a links, so it can therefore be something of a shock to discover that Lytham is over a mile from the sea and indeed is separated from it by rows of red-bricked houses. Nevertheless, the turf

is of the right stuff – sandy based and fast running – and a links it is.

This shot from behind the 9th green exemplifies the special characteristics of golf at Lytham. The houses and the railway line – which can come into play on several holes on the front nine – are perhaps two of the images that most set Lytham apart from its championship neighbour along the coast at Birkdale. Another is the lack of high

dunes. Lytham is not a flamboyant course; rather a down-to-earth examination of the game which becomes a bit more than that when the wind is up and the pressure is on.

The 9th proves the point perfectly. In the 1974 Open, Gary Player held a five-shot lead at the halfway stage and was still four clear of the pack as he stood on the slightly elevated tee of this hole. He then dumped his ball into one of the bunkers and needed

two blows to extract himself from the sand. Ten minutes later he had lost his lead altogether but, dogged as ever, he went on to win his third Open that week.

Royal Lytham's most recent appearance on centre stage occurred when it hosted the 1988 championship. As he had been here in 1979, Seve Ballesteros was the winner. His closing 65, six under par, was one of the greatest scores ever produced in the final round of a major championship, and it included a stretch from the 6th to the 11th which he played in six under par, with four birdies and an eagle. The only hole where he had to settle for par was this one. The 9th, like the entire course, demonstrates that it's not necessary to be flash to have class.

ᴿOYAL MELBOURNE has two outstanding 18-hole golf courses. First came the West, fashioned with the old faithful tools of horse and scoop under the direction of Dr Alister Mackenzie, the Scotsman who would later leave an unforgettable mark at two of the greatest courses in the United States, Cypress Point and Augusta National. After Mack-enzie had departed for North America, Alex Russell, who had assisted Mackenzie in his work, laid out the East Course. When the two are merged, as they are for championships such as the Australian Open, and interna-tional events like the 1988 World Cup, they combine to form one of the best courses in the world and surely the best in the south-ern hemisphere.

There are those who are prepared to go further than that. Two winners of major championships, Ben Crenshaw and Greg Norman, have declared it to be their favourite course anywhere, and they and others of Royal Melbourne's advocates would not dispute that the 5th is one of its strongest holes.

It typifies the entire course, with the appearance of a British heathland layout but with many of the characteristics of a fast-

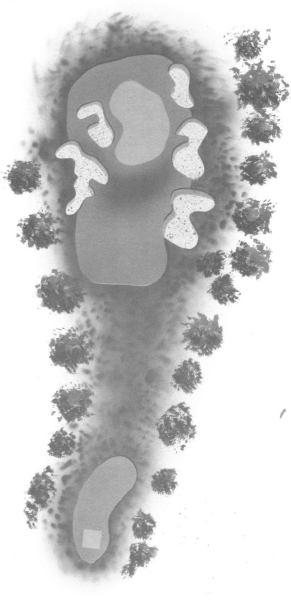

running links. Royal Melbourne does not suffer for want of sand, and the bunkers protecting this upraised green are no more or less ferocious than most to be encountered during the round. The same holds true for the greens, which will in fact only hold a perfect shot and, though true to putt, are usually fast enough to make putting into a bunker a devastating possibility. A severely canted edge to the front of this green means that a marginally underhit shot is inevitably condemned to roll back down the slope towards the tee, while a putt from the back has to contend with a deceptively steep downward incline. The sand belt of the Melbourne area is well endowed with excellent golf courses, but Royal Melbourne has no peer among them.

5th at Royal Portrush (Dunluce Course)

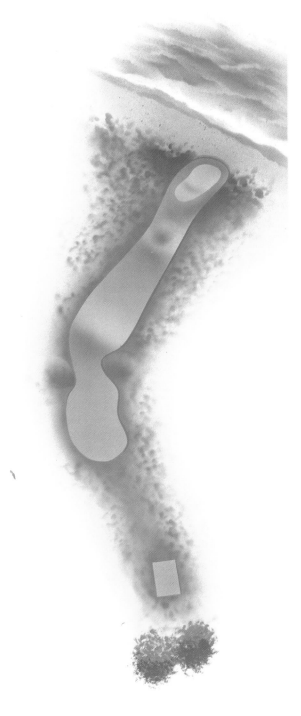

386 YARDS, PAR-4

*W*HILE ONE WOULD not wish to be playing one's second shot to the 5th green at Portrush from this spot, this picture illustrates how much Portrush is a welcome exception to a few other British links. As Bernard Darwin's eloquent pen once noted, it is 'a remarkable thing that though golf courses are often in lovely places it fre-quently so happens that the beauties of the landscape are to be seen from anywhere except the course. Who, for instance, ever heard of a self-respecting seaside course where one could get a view of the sea!'

The beauty of the backdrop to this green has also been the source of its biggest scourge. The Antrim coastline of Northern Ireland is regularly battered by severe winds off the ocean, and that glorious sandy

beach has reclaimed some of the cliffside upon which this section of the Dunluce Course is built. The club has therefore installed gabions to fortify its territory and thereby to safeguard the integrity of a magnificent hole. And the precipice upon which this green rests does not merely have scenic impact. As Darwin observed, this is 'one of those holes where for some inscrutable reason it is very easy to be either too far or too short'. And as awkward as the approach to the plateau green is, the drive is no easy matter either, since it has to negotiate the sharp bend to the right of the fairway in the landing area.

Portrush is a genuinely historic course. It is the only place outside England or Scotland to have hosted the Open Championship. That was in 1951, and Max Faulkner of England was the winner. Four years previously, a former caddie at Portrush, Fred Daly, had become the first Irishman to carry off the title. The club's connection with the ladies' game is equally strong. The Hezlet sisters, who dominated the female amateur scene at the turn of the century, hailed from Portrush, and the course was the scene for Lady Margaret Scott to complete a hat-trick of victories in the first three Ladies' Open Amateur Championships.

6th at Royal St George's

N 1894 ROYAL ST GEORGE'S at Sandwich in Kent became the first English course to hold the Open Championship, but it has since been immortalized by two eminent authors for reasons which have little or nothing to do with its calibre as a championship test.

This photograph shows the short 6th, the notorious 'Maiden' hole; so named on account of a Himalayan and bunker-strewn mound which golfers in the days of yore had to clear with their tee shots but which, to the chagrin of the traditionalists, no longer has to be carried from the new tee in the right-hand centre of the picture. Bernard Darwin, perhaps the finest of all British golf writers, was among those who regretted the march of progress, but it was his pen that unforgettably captured the atmosphere of St George's when he wrote: 'The long strip of turf on the way to the 7th hole [above the green to the left] that stretches between the sandhills and the sea; a fine spring day, with the larks singing as they seem to sing nowhere else; the sun shining on the waters of Pegwell Bay and lighting up the white cliffs in the distance; this is nearly my idea of Heaven as is to be attained on any earthly links.'

The 6th played an important part in one of the most famous golf matches ever fought – the fictional contest between James Bond and Auric Goldfinger, created by Ian Fleming and staged over a course thinly disguised as Royal St Marks. Fleming cheekily called his 6th hole 'the Virgin'. Bond's tee shot finished 20 feet from the pin; Goldfinger's found a heel-mark in the deep bunker nearest the camera. 'Bond walked over to his ball and listened to the larks', wrote Fleming, no doubt with a nod in the direction of Darwin. Goldfinger then, of course, cheated, improving his lie and saving his par. A shaken Bond three-putted to go one down, but was stirred into making sure that he would not lose. He didn't.

8th at Royal Troon

126 YARDS, PAR-3

NOT SURPRISINGLY, this is the shortest hole on the Open Championship rota. From a raised tee, it may only need a wedge to put the ball on the green of the 'Postage Stamp'. On the other hand, if the wind is off the waters of the Firth of Clyde, it may require as much as a 3-iron.

The most celebrated shot ever played from this tee was with a 5-iron. It was hit by Gene Sarazen in the 1973 Open, on the 50th anniversary of his debut in the championship. At Troon in 1923 he had failed to get through the qualifying rounds – a humiliation for a man who was the reigning US Open champion. In 1973, aged 71, he had a hole-in-one at the 8th in the first round to the cheers of an appreciative gallery and to the amazement of not only himself but also

of millions of television viewers. He punched his 5-iron into the soft breeze, the ball landed 20 feet short of the flag and rolled in for his ace. This romantic script was not followed by another American past winner of the Open, Arnold Palmer, who had been victorious at Troon in 1962. He showed how hard the 8th can play by taking a seven on it in the second round, a day that witnessed Sarazen hole out from a bunker for a birdie.

Two miracles in two days! Inevitably Sarazen failed to survive the halfway cut, but he left Ayrshire with memories which neither he nor his audience would ever forget.

As Palmer proved, the 8th is not to be trifled with. A German amateur named Herman Tissies found that out with a vengeance in the 1950 Open when he sampled most of the bunkers on offer in the course of running

up a 15 on the hole. By the time he left the green he realized why the 8th is called the Postage Stamp. With a club in the hand, it can seem about the size of one. But in another way the nickname is inappropriate. Unlike the sort that goes on an envelope, this postage stamp is not easily licked.

17th at St Andrews (Old Course)

461 YARDS, PAR-4

HE 17TH AT ST ANDREWS, the 'Road Hole', is one of the oldest par-4s in the world. It is also, according to Severiano Ballesteros, the hardest. To reach the haven of the fairway in the near foreground of this picture, the drive has to flirt with the grounds of the Old Course Hotel, formerly a railway yard but still out-of-bounds. That requires nerve and

talent, and even then one is faced with having to play a draw with a long iron in along the green, a shot which, down the ages, has taken a terrible toll.

St Andrews is known throughout the world as the home of golf. Records show that the game has been played over the land that now constitutes the Old Course at least since 1552. Perhaps the course's most distinctive characteristic is its huge double

greens – the 17th is one of only four holes not to have one. And what an elusive target its single green has been to generations of golfers, not least in the 23 Open Championships that St Andrews hosted between 1873 and 1984.

An incident from the 1885 Open illustrates the point perfectly. David Ayton spent some time flitting between the Road Bunker, which Bernard Darwin described as 'eating its way into the very vitals' of the green, and the road itself which runs across the back of the green in front of the stone wall. Ayton left the hole with an 11 on his card. An overly powerful second shot onto the road cost Tom Watson his chance of catching Ballesteros in the 1984 championship. Another five-time Open winner, J.H. Taylor, once took 13 here. Japan's Tommy Nakajima suffered a nine in the 1978 Open. Having adopted the cautious, sensible policy of playing for the front right portion of the green in the hope of getting into the hole – which is always cut behind that evil bunker on major occasions – in two more strokes, Nakajima then putted his ball into the sand and took four swipes to emerge. As that incident demonstrated, this is a hole where going for the flag with a putter can be dangerous.

11th at St Mellion (Jack Nicklaus Course)

203 YARDS, PAR-3

Jack Nicklaus's phenomenal achievements as a player, including a record of 20 major championships which will surely never be equalled, mean that his place in the annals of the game is assured. But it has never been a Nicklaus policy to rest on his laurels; he didn't get where he has by doing that. Now he is attempting the seemingly impossible – a word not in Jack's lexicon – in trying to make as big a name for himself in history as a golf course architect. Some of his work in the United States is featured in these pages. St Mellion was his first project in the British Isles, as Nicklaus, like so many other prominent American course architects of the modern era, realized that Europe represents the most burgeoning market for golf course development in the world.

In this neck of Cornwall, in the comparatively remote south-west of England, Nicklaus ran into something fairly alien to him in his playing career – controversy. British architects were understandably somewhat envious of what eventually turned out to be his £3 million budget, and critical of the way in which Nicklaus had spent so much of that money in rearranging the topography. Whether that is sour grapes, professional jealousy or justified comment may be a matter of opinion. What is undeniable is that this hole can leave a bitter taste in one's mouth.

From way back in the hillside, even the substantial elevation of the tee does little to alter the opinion that the 11th is not going to be an easy hole to leave while savouring the sweet taste of success. When the course had its professional baptism at the 1987 Ladies British Open, the women found the hole tough enough from 140 yards out. This short hole is not only not that short from the back tees but it is also one on which you don't want to be short from anywhere.

18th at Shinnecock Hills

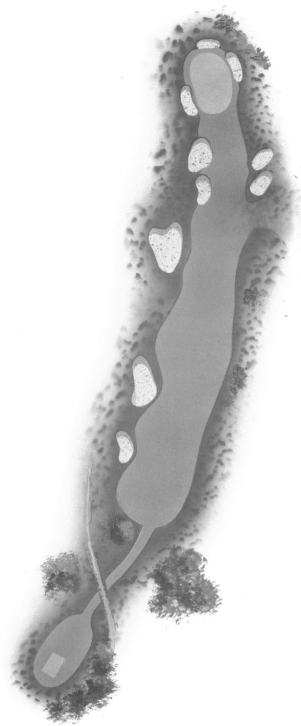

426 YARDS, PAR-4

SHINNECOCK HILLS is arguably the least contrived golf course in the United States – hardly surprising, really, considering that the original was laid out in 1891 by Willie Dunn, one of the *émigré* Scotsmen who made a handsome living in those days by showing the Americans what golf was all about. Shinnecock hosted the second US Open in 1896, although it did not hold another until a further 90 years had elapsed and substantial modifications had been undertaken. The chief reason for this multi-generation gap was concern that the course and its environs would not be able to cope with the pressures of putting on a major championship in the modern age, but the local community held up under the weight of the traffic and the course held up magnificently under the

assault of the best golfers in the world.

Willie Dunn was no doubt surprised and delighted when he first cast his eyes over the site to find that it was not unlike the terrain to be found along the coastline of his native land. It is bound by the Atlantic Ocean on one side and by Long Island Sound on the other. It is actually some two miles from the sea – and, incidentally, about 90 miles east of New York City – but the natural flow of the land and the firm turf upon which the course was constructed conspire to bestow an air of links golf upon Shinnecock.

The closing hole reflects these qualities, not least in the sinuous manner in which the fairway approaches the green, which is slightly upraised from the ground immediately before it. The 18th is a suitably tough finale to this marvellous course. The drive must carry far enough to reach the point where the fairway turns to the left for the second shot. At the 1986 US Open, that problem was exacerbated by some typically penal USGA rough which threatened the errant tee shot. Ray Floyd's winning total was 279, one under par – proof that Shinnecock may be old but is by no means past it.

18th at Shoal Creek

T WASN'T CHEAP for Jack Nicklaus to cut a championship golf course from out of this tract of wildlife-infested wilderness 25 miles south of Birmingham, Alabama. The man who employed him to do it, the owner of Shoal Creek, was a local millionaire called Hall Thompson, who wasn't really distressed at the costs incurred and was positively delighted when Shoal Creek was chosen as the venue for the 1984 US PGA Championship. So successful was that occasion that the tournament will return to Shoal Creek in 1990.

Among the many species of original inhabitants of the land on which the course now stands are rattlesnakes, but though they were sometimes spotted during the 1984 US PGA Championship, most of the venom that week was to be found in the thick rough that lined every fairway, and quite a bit of damage was perpetrated by the 18th hole, which – looking back towards the tee from behind the green – occupies the centre portion of this picture to the left of the lake.

Nick Faldo was only one shot off the lead playing the hole in the second round before the rough ensnared his drive and the

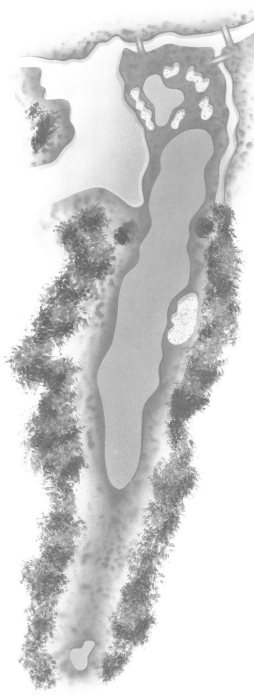

446 YARDS, PAR-4

water and three putts saddled him with an eight. The next day, tournament leader Lee Trevino knocked his approach into the lake here and took a six, reducing his advantage to one stroke. But for him it didn't matter. It was only one of three holes all week on which he strayed over par, and on the final afternoon he sank a putt of six yards on the 18th green for a birdie three and a winning 15-under-par total of 273. It was the second time that Trevino had broken 70 in all four rounds of a major championship (the other was at the 1968 US Open) and only the fourth time in all that that feat had ever been accomplished. For Shoal Creek, it was golfing history at the first attempt.

3rd at Spanish Bay

405 YARDS, PAR-4

THE LINKS AT SPANISH BAY is the full name for this breathtaking place, one of four courses on California's Monterey Peninsula to be included in this book. As ever, the connotations inherent in that word 'links' are slightly misleading, but of all the American courses which incorporate the term into their name it may be that Spanish Bay has the most legitimate claim to the honour. The course was designed by Robert Trent Jones Jnr, with not a little help from his friends Tom Watson and Frank (Sandy) Tatum, who has already appeared in these pages bestowing praise of the highest order upon Cypress Point. The recognition Spanish Bay has received since its opening in 1987 has been partly because of the fescue grasses, which Jones has assiduously in-

sisted should be used to enhance the ambience of links golf, and partly despite them. Persuading the fescue to take on the exposed Pacific coastline has not been a simple task, but then Spanish Bay was no straightforward project. Jones and his distinguished collaborators paid meticulous attention to detail, such as relocating the indigenous sandhills to be more in sympathy with the feel of a genuine links, and

erecting fresh dunes and building bunkers where it was deemed they would have existed naturally had the terrain lent itself to being moulded by the elements, especially by the wind off the ocean, as has been the case down the centuries at courses like St Andrews. A bonus of this care for the landscape has been a revitalization of the environment, particularly the plant life.

The 3rd is one of several tremendous

par-4s at Spanish Bay, with the sea providing an enticing panorama and the fairway demanding a drive to the right side unless one is to flirt with the bunkers which punctuate the near corner of the gentle bend to the left that sends the hole onto a green nestling in a hollow. And while the weather looks benign enough here, Spanish Bay can be battered by winds strong enough to sink an Armada.

2nd at Spyglass Hill

ROBERT LOUIS STEVENSON was not only responsible for heaping glorious and unqualified praise upon Pebble Beach but it is from his novel *Treasure Island* that Spyglass Hill, Pebble's neighbour along California's Monterey Peninsula, and its holes take their name. As Pebble Beach, Cypress Point and Spanish Bay have spectacularly emphasized already, this is tremendous golfing territory. Spyglass is a public course like Pebble Beach and its opening and most dramatic holes are almost adjoining Cypress Point. Spyglass Hill shares with Pebble and Cypress the honour of co-hosting the AT & T National Pro-Am on the US tour each January or February, the event originally called, with a little more glamour and romance, the Bing Crosby National Pro-Am until the American telephone company assumed sponsorship. But whoever's name has been attached to the tournament, Spyglass has invariably proved to be the toughest of the three venues for both the professionals and their celebrity partners.

This photograph from behind the 2nd green shows the sandy wasteland and scrub that stamp the character of those wonderful early holes at Spyglass, such as this one and

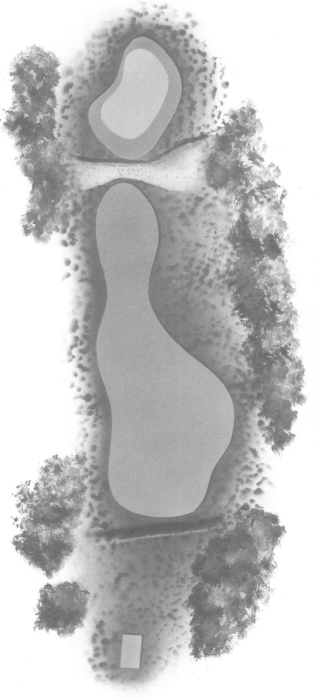

350 YARDS, PAR-4

the 4th and 5th in the background. The holes take their names from a mixture of Scottish tradition and Stevenson's imagination. The 2nd is 'Billy Bones'. The tee is at the top right of the picture and most players will probably elect to drive with an iron. Going with a wood is unnecessary given that one has to find the fairway, which narrows towards the green, and that the hole is not long. Assuming the first step has been negotiated safely, the next problem is to hit and hold an elevated green which tends to throw the ball to the right and is obviously not short of protection in front.

If you think that all this is to exaggerate the difficulties of the start at Spyglass, consider the tale of two doctors who once ran through three dozen balls by the time they had completed the 6th. It was not so much a spyglass they needed as a homing device.

5th at Sunningdale (Old Course)

O F ONE GOLF COURSE could be said to epitomize all that is best about inland golf in the British Isles then Sunningdale is it. It is invariably in good condition. Its fairways are firm and crisp, its greens quick and true. Pine, birch and heather combine to paint one of the prettiest pictures in golfdom, and the scene depicted here is one of the most widely recognized golf settings in the world: a veritable classic in a rural paradise only 25 miles from central London.

The elevated green of the short 4th is in the foreground. The 5th tee is at the same level, just out of shot to the left; the 5th green is beyond the pond located on the right edge of the fairway. In the far distance the 6th hole cuts an alley through the tree line. The natural assumption is that Sunningdale was laid out in a forest, but in fact when Willie Park Jnr built it around the turn of the century few of the trees were in existence. Most were added by Harry Colt, the master architect who was appointed secretary of the club in 1901. At under 6600 yards, Sunningdale has been known to take a battering from today's professionals, such as when Ian Woosnam won the 1988 European Open with a total of 260, but generally

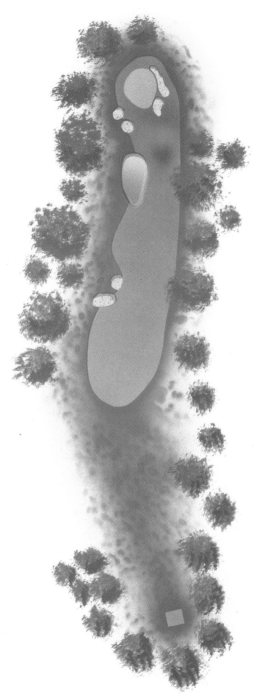

fears that the power of the modern players will bludgeon its subtleties into irrelevance prove to be ill-founded. And for the club golfer, Sunningdale is simply gorgeous.

The 5th is not the hardest four at Sunningdale, although there are plenty of members and professionals who have found the fairway elusive and the pond eager to grasp a mis-hit approach. The 5th was one of the six holes birdied by Bobby Jones, the greatest amateur and maybe the greatest player the game has ever known, when he shot a 66 during a qualifying competition for the 1926 Open Championship – a stunning score in those days. That established a tradition for admirable achievements at Sunningdale, a club that can also break down tradition. When it was awarded the 1987 Walker Cup match, it became the first British inland course to be so honoured.

18th at the Tournament Players Club

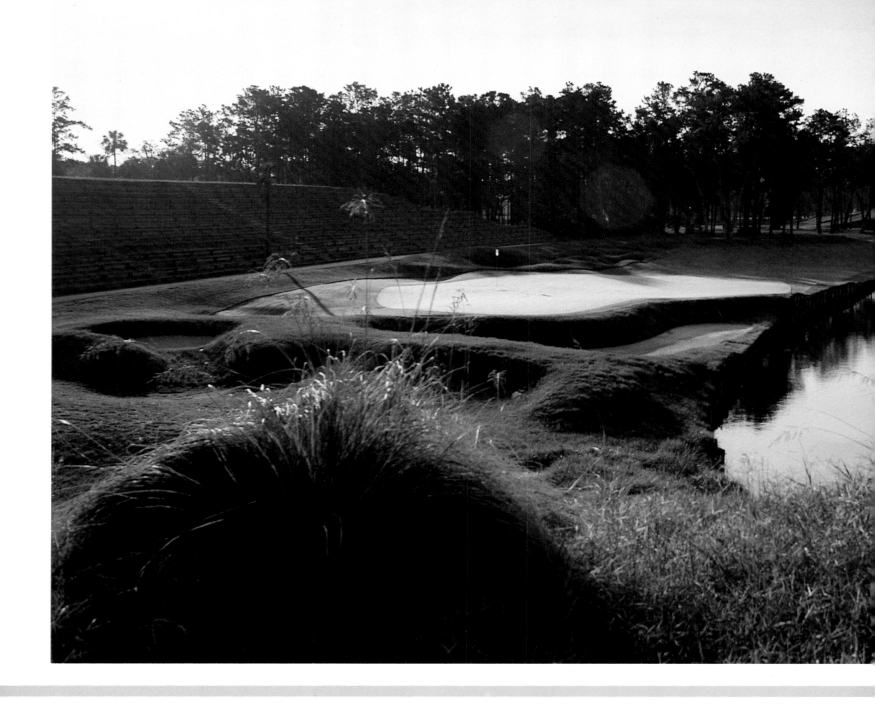

O F ALL THE GOLF COURSES built around the world in the 1980s, none has had such an impact as that at the Tournament Players Club at Sawgrass in north-eastern Florida. It has simultaneously been the most imitated and the most reviled, although one of Pete Dye's subsequent projects (see PGA West) has deflected some of the flak away from his original 'stadium course'. Also, despite the architect's reluctance, modifications have been made since this course humbled many of the world's best golfers during its first staging of the Tournament Players Championship – now simply the Players Championship, golf's putative 'fifth major' – in 1982. Then the likes of Jack Nicklaus complained that the greens were convex, tending to repel rather than retain a good shot.

Today the TPC course may be a little fairer but it is still fierce. The closing hole emphasizes its characteristics – deep bunkers, grassy hollows and plenty of water. This photograph also shows the spectator mounds constructed beside the green and down towards the tee, from where the fans have an uninterrupted sight of the professionals executing one of the most pressurized drives in golf. The hole is unashamedly

440 YARDS, PAR-4

modelled on the 18th at Pebble Beach, though the latter is a par-5. A hook is obviously to be avoided at all costs, but a timid push to the right may leave the green out of range, or even out of sight behind the trees.

In the 1983 championship, John Cook needed a par here to force a playoff with Hal Sutton, but he hooked his drive into the water and that was that. The previous year the lake had lured in more than just a golf ball at the prize-giving ceremony. Jerry Pate, who had secured the title with a birdie at the last, celebrated by diving in for a swim – after first having pushed in US PGA Tour Commissioner Deane Beman and that man Dye. On behalf of his fellow-pros, Pate thus ensured that while Dye might be unrepentant he would at least have wet feet.

16th at Turnberry (Ailsa Course)

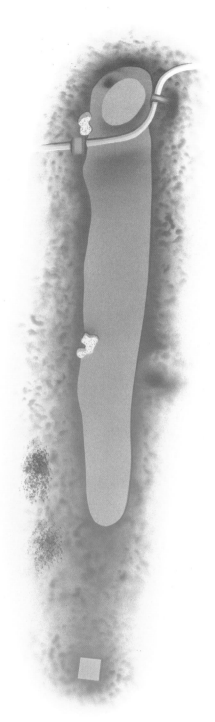

409 YARDS, PAR-4

TURNBERRY ON A SUMMER'S EVENING is one of the most heavenly places on earth, a feeling captured in this photograph along with a distant sight (on the far left-hand point of the horizon) of a portion of Ailsa Craig, the gigantic rock which rises from the sea and gives its name to this course. The waters of the Firth of Clyde are, at times, right beside the course, closer to the links than on any of the other current hosts to the Open Championship.

On the other hand, in foul weather Turnberry can bear an uncomfortable resemblance to Hell. It was that way for the first three days of the 1986 Open, when Greg Norman took hold of the championship with a second round of 63, seven under par, which Tom Watson later described as the

greatest round ever played in a tournament in which he was a competitor. The elements had been kind beyond belief to the Ayrshire coast nine years earlier when Watson himself had won Turnberry's first and his second Open after a thrilling duel with Jack Nicklaus over the final 36 holes. Watson shot 65–65 to Nicklaus's 65–66 in what many experts reckon might have been the greatest major championship in history.

Norman's effort in his *annus mirabilis* was less memorable because he strolled away with the title by five shots. During that scarcely credible 63, Norman birdied the 16th from six feet after an 8-iron approach. The next day, his closest pursuer, Tommy Nakajima of Japan, hit his 2-iron second shot through the rain-lashed gale into the 'Wee Burn', from which the hole takes its name, in front of the green. He took a double-bogey

and finished the day a stroke behind Norman. His challenge the following afternoon was stillborn when he four-putted at the first, but it may be that the man from the east saw his hopes of the Open go west with that six at the 16th.

7th at Vale do Lobo (Yellow Course)

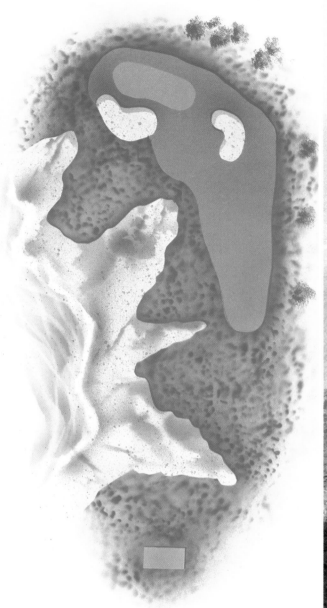

238 YARDS, PAR-3

'V ALE DO LOBO' IS PORTUGUESE for 'Valley of the Wolf'. In many respects this course along the golden Atlantic coastline of southern Portugal could be appropriately renamed Land of the Bandit. The courses of the Algarve, as this glorious region is known, are regularly packed with golfers from all over Europe who have come in search of sun, cheap food and wine, plus a few rounds of golf with a set of clubs and, frequently, an indecently generous handicap. Some of these courses also possess fairways which are narrow enough to do justice to the US Open, although their confines are not delineated by penal rough but by whitewashed holiday villas and apartments which often lurk so close to the action among the umbrella pines that the most

likely water hazard to be found by an errant shot is somebody's swimming pool.

However, the above is not to suggest that Vale do Lobo and its companions are merely golfing goat tracks, and there is no mistaking the identity of the chief water hazard on this hole, the celebrated 7th on Vale do Lobo's Yellow nine. The 27 holes here – the other loops are called the Green and the Orange – were designed by the late Sir Henry Cotton, who was also responsible for Penina, another popular course in an area which, along with Spain's Costa del Sol, dominates the European golf holiday market.

The reputation of this hole extends far beyond Europe. It is a tremendously tough par-3, but at the same time a great hole for the hacker as well as for the professional. It is easy to make four by playing safely to the right off the tee; indeed, such prudence may bring a par. But even the most humble practitioner of the game is inclined to feel that he hasn't come all the way to Vale do Lobo just to chicken out, so with knuckles whitening and heart pounding he will aim over the chasms in the eroded sandstone cliffs and go for the green. And if he makes it, it will have made his day.

16th at Walton Heath (Old Course)

WALTON IS A BEAUTIFUL, if at times blasted, heath. For the members it is a par-5 off the back tee, but it is frequently played as a formidable 478-yard par-4, and it is as a tough two-shotter that the professionals tackle it when they have the pleasure of visiting what is one of the many great tests of golf to the south of London. Then the course is a composite layout which plucks three holes off the New Course to supplement 15 from the Old. This hole remains the 16th even with that juggling, although it used to be the 17th back in the days when Bernard Darwin commented: 'The second shot is the thing ... to the right the face of the hill is excavated in a deep and terrible bunker, and a ball ever so slightly sliced will run into that bunker as sure as fate. To the left there is heather extending almost to the edge of the green, and, in avoiding the right-hand bunker, we may very likely die an even more painful death in the heather.'

One does not have to look anywhere else but at this photograph to see what Darwin meant. The long shot home is indeed fraught with danger, yet Walton Heath not only demands excellence, it rewards it. This was never more emphatically demonstrated than

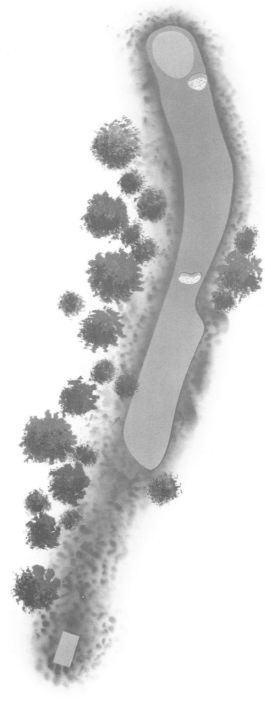

at the 1981 Ryder Cup, where Tom Kite defeated Sandy Lyle in the last day's singles to help the United States retain the trophy. Lyle lost the match on this green despite having made eight birdies. Kite had made ten, including one here.

Walton Heath shares with Sunningdale the staging of the European Open each autumn, and the event began at Walton in 1978 with a thrilling climax on this hole. The American, Bobby Wadkins, hit a 3-iron to within a yard of the cup to set up a birdie three which gave him the title at the first hole of a sudden-death playoff. But do not be deceived by such heroics. Five is a far more common score than three on this hole, and it has been ever since the course was opened in 1904. Five-time Open champion James Braid was the club's first professional. Walton Heath is a place fit for champions.

16th at Waterville

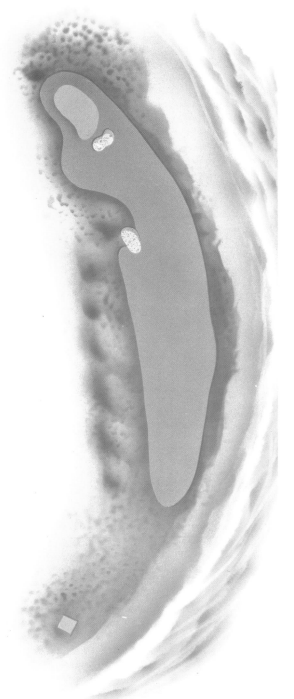

366 YARDS, PAR-4

FROM BEHIND THE GREEN, it is easy to understand why the 16th hole at Waterville in Co. Kerry, in the glorious golfing country of south-west Ireland, used to be called 'Round the Bend'. The name was changed in 1979 to 'Liam's Ace' on account of the achievement of the club's professional, Liam Higgins. He had a hole-in-one here on the way to establishing a new course record of 65, seven under par. It isn't hard to see why it was decided to rechristen the hole, but it isn't easy to imagine how a man could hit the ball that far and that straight even given that as the crow flies – or as Higgins' ball flew – the carry is nearer 300 yards.

Higgins, obviously, is a prodigious hitter. At Waterville, that comes in handy. The course measures 7257 yards from the back

plates. The 16th is one of several fine holes which form a marvellous climax to a round at Waterville; an experience played out against a setting of sturdy, shaggy sandhills. The 16th is bounded by those on the one side and by the Atlantic Ocean on the other, and assuming that you are not Liam Higgins or Greg Norman, the drive has to be sufficiently far and sufficiently to the right side of the fairway if the green is to be in view for the second shot. Too far right means into the sea, but there is some consolation. The Atlantic has been defined as a lateral water hazard – which means that one can take a drop under penalty on either side of it!

The wind at Waterville is inevitably a further problem with which one has to contend. It can vary from a zephyr to a storm, and its effect is often disguised by those looming dunes, particularly on the back nine – the more appealing and the more demanding half – where the majesty of Royal Birkdale is brought to mind. Despite its sandhills and its proximity to the sea, the turf at Waterville is more parkland than linksland in its character, but that does not detract from the overall impact. After all, if a guy can hole out with a driver, the place must be touched by magic.

13th at Wentworth (West Course)

ENTWORTH is just two miles down the road towards London from Sunningdale. It tends to play rather longer than its Surrey neighbour, and not simply because it is indeed nearly 400 yards longer. The soil is not so permeable, so Wentworth in the wet is a searching examination of power as well as of prowess. That is the challenge that has faced the best professional golfers in the world every autumn since 1964, when the World Matchplay Championship was inaugurated. The West Course, 'the Burma Road', is its permanent home, a circumstance which has been of benefit to both the club and the tournament.

In common with most of the two-shot holes at Wentworth, the green on the 13th is not in view from the tee. The hole curves round to the left, thereby demanding that the drive must skirt the two bunkers which protect the right side of the fairway if it is to offer a clear line into the flag. It's a matter of either that or else the golfer having the ability to fashion a high, wide draw around and maybe over the tall evergreens on the left with the approach shot.

This green has a reputation as being perhaps the hardest of all 18 to read. That

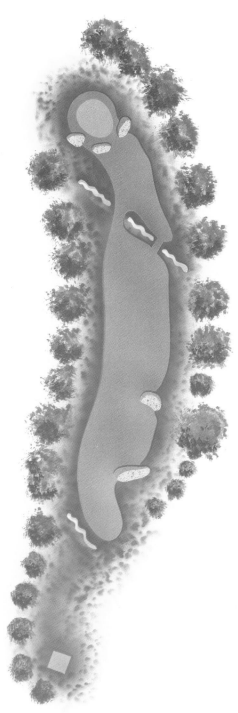

may indeed be so, but the received wisdom was defied in one of the most celebrated episodes ever enacted on it. In a semi-final of the 1965 World Matchplay, Gary Player came to this hole three down to Tony Lema. He had been seven down earlier in the long day, but it seemed his revival might be ended here when Lema knocked in a long putt to save an unlikely par. Not a bit of it. Player holed from 10 feet for a three to

reduce the arrears still further. It is an old golfing maxim that 'two up with five to play never wins', and it was to hold true again. Lema was beaten at the first extra hole as Player completed one of the most remarkable comebacks in the history of matchplay golf. No wonder he describes this as 'one of my favourite holes'. He, a five-time winner of the championship, is a cumulative ten under par for the event on the 13th.

10th at Winged Foot (West Course)

WINGED FOOT, in Mamaroneck, less than an hour's drive from the heart of New York City, has held four US Open Championships. The most recent of these, in 1984, produced a stirring fourth-round climax. Greg Norman faced a seemingly impossible downhill, breaking putt of 30 feet on the 18th green to finish on 276. He holed it. As he celebrated,

Fuzzy Zoeller, who now needed a par to tie, watched from back on the fairway in the belief that Norman's putt was for a birdie and 275. Taking a white towel from his caddie, he waved it in mock surrender. His sporting gesture was rewarded when he parred the hole and swept home by eight shots in the ensuing playoff.

Winged Foot was built by Albert Tillinghast, who in 1923 was instructed by the

property owners, the New York Athletic Club, to 'give us a man-sized course'. His response was to bring an enviable array of trees into play and to construct several upraised greens and guard them with man-sized bunkers. The greens thus represent an elusive target – they can be tricky to hold with merely a short pitch – and once on them it is not easy to read the subtle slopes.

The 10th is not only arguably the best

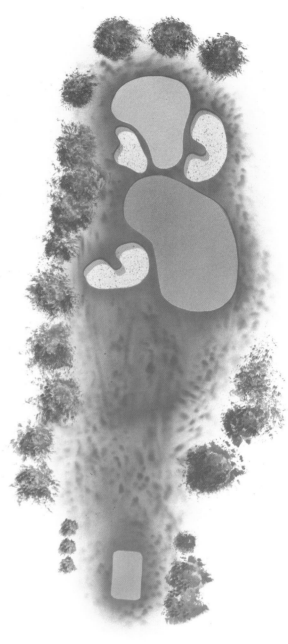

hole on the course but it also embodies the principal features which mean that while Winged Foot may appear to be rather prosaic, it is instead a masterpiece. At 190 yards, this short hole demands a long iron from the tee. Mindful of a house standing just the other side of the tree line, Ben Hogan once described it as 'a 3-iron into some guy's bedroom'. Anywhere except on the green is in trouble. There is a bunker short to catch the gross mis-hit; two cavernous traps left and right; and out-of-bounds over the back. The green is tilted from back-to-front, which looks inviting from the tee but it makes it inordinately awkward to lay a chip, or even a putt, close. It is also distressingly straightforward to blast from one of those two steep bunkers into the other. Tillinghast called it the best par-3 he ever designed.

155

18th at Woodhall Spa

AUGUSTA NATIONAL is a tough act to follow. The home of the Masters provided a fittingly grandiose start to this book. By comparison, Woodhall Spa, a course situated in a pleasant small town in the heart of the Lincolnshire countryside, may seem to be a rather understated way with which to close. But in fact, just as Augusta National

has claims to be the finest course in the United States, so Woodhall Spa is not short of adherents who would declare it to be the best inland course in the British Isles.

Woodhall Spa has not hosted major professional tournaments – its remote location would preclude that – but it is frequently chosen to host amateur events of distinction. And Woodhall Spa is distinctive: a sandy-soiled, pine-clad, heather-covered

tract of land in an area that is renowned for its featureless landscape. So instead of bleak boredom, the qualities possessed by the golf course of this rural spa town make it the quintessential specimen of the genre affectionately classified as an inland links.

The 18th exemplifies the character of Woodhall Spa. From this, the 'Brabazon Tee' (so named on account of its use when the club has staged the Brabazon Trophy), it is a

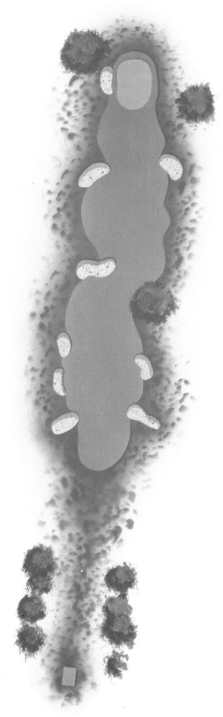

short par-5, but it demands everything in terms of accuracy. The flag can be seen in the far distance, but from the tee one is inclined to be imbued with a feeling of claustrophobia rather than confidence, and the fairway seems an unreasonably small target. Assuming the dauntingly narrow gap between the foliage has been safely negotiated with the drive, one's ball will hopefully stay left of the giant oak which stands like a sentinel on the right. The fast-running fairway is intermittently protected all the way to the green by bunkers every bit as satanic and plentiful as those on another English 'inland links', Ganton. They, too, are typical of Woodhall Spa, and on this hole as on its other 17 they can wreck a score. That would be a sorry way to complete a round at Woodhall Spa, although the course itself is a suitable way to conclude this book.

Bibliography

In addition to drawing on material contained in the books listed here, the author has been greatly assisted by information published in the British magazine *Golf World* and the American magazine *Golf Digest*.

Darwin, Bernard: *The Golf Courses of the British Isles* (Duckworth, London 1910 and Storey Communications/Ailsa Inc. New York 1988)

Davis, William H. and the Editors of *Golf Digest*: *Great Golf Courses of the World* (Golf Digest, New York 1974); 100 *Greatest Golf Courses And Then Some* (Golf Digest/Tennis Inc. New York 1982)

Fleming, Ian: *Goldfinger* (Jonathan Cape, London 1959)

Green, Robert *Golf: An Illustrated History of the Game* (Collins Willow, London 1987)

Gregston, Gene: *Hogan, The Man Who Played for Glory* (Prentice Hall Inc, New Jersey 1978)

Longhurst, Henry: *My Life and Soft Times* (Cassell & Co, London 1971)

Macdonald, Charles Blair: *Scotland's Gift – Golf* (Charles Scribner's Sons, New York 1928 and Ailsa Inc, New York 1985)

Mackenzie, Alister: *Dr Mackenzie's Golf Architecture* (Simpkin, Marshall, Hamilton and Kent, London 1920 and Grant Books, Droitwich 1982)

Morgan, Brian: *A World Portrait of Golf* (Aurum Press, London 1988)

Palmer, Arnold (with William Barry Furlong): *Go For Broke!* (William Kimber, London 1974)

Parsons, Iain (Editor): *The World Atlas of Golf* (Mitchell Beazley, London 1976)

Shelly, Warner: *Pine Valley Golf Club, A Chronicle* (Pine Valley Golf Club, New Jersey 1982)

Wind, Herbert Warren: *The Lure of Golf* (Heinemann, London 1971)

Index of courses by country

Australia
Royal Melbourne, *Melbourne, Victoria*

Bolivia
La Paz, *La Paz*

Canada
Banff Springs, *Banff, Alberta*

China
Chung Shan Hot Spring, *Guangdong Province*

Dominican Republic
Casa de Campo, *Casa de Campo*

England
Belfry, The, *Sutton Coldfield, West Midlands*
Ganton, *North Yorkshire*
Royal Birkdale, *Southport, Merseyside*
Royal Lytham and St Annes, *Lytham St Annes, Lancashire*
Royal St George's, *Sandwich, Kent*
St Mellion, *Saltash, Cornwall*
Sunningdale, *Sunningdale, Surrey*
Walton Heath, *Tadworth, Surrey*
Wentworth, *Virginia Water, Surrey*
Woodhall Spa, *Lincolnshire*

France
Chantilly, *Chantilly, nr Paris*
Morfontaine, *Mortefontaine, nr Paris*

Holland
Kennemer, *Zandvoort*

Hong Kong
Royal Hong Kong, *Fanling*

Jamaica
Rose Hall, *Montego Bay*

Japan
New St Andrews, *nr Tokyo*

Morocco
Royal Dar-es-Salam, *Rabat*

New Zealand
Paraparaumu Beach, *Paraparaumu, nr Wellington, North Island*

Northern Ireland
Royal County Down, *Newcastle, Co. Down*
Royal Portrush, *Co. Antrim*

Portugal
Vale do Lobo, *Quinta do Lago*

Republic of Ireland
Ballybunion, *Co. Kerry*
Portmarnock, *Dublin*
Waterville, *Co. Kerry*

Scotland
Carnoustie, *Angus*
Gleneagles, *Auchterarder, Perthshire*
Muirfield, *Gullane, Lothian*
Royal Dornoch, *Sutherland*
Royal Troon, *Ayrshire*
St Andrews, *Fife*
Turnberry, *Ayrshire*

South Africa
Mowbray, *Cape Town*

Spain
El Saler, *nr Valencia*

Sweden
Falsterbo, *Skanör, nr Malmo*

United States of America
Augusta National, *Augusta, Georgia*
Baltusrol, *Springfield, New Jersey*
Bay Hill, *Orlando, Florida*
Cherry Hill, *Englewood, nr Denver, Colorado*
Colonial, *Fort Worth, Texas*
Cypress Point, *Pebble Beach, California*
Desert Highlands, *Scottsdale, Arizona*
Firestone, *Akron, Ohio*
Grand Cypress, *Orlando, Florida*
Harbour Town, *Hilton Head Island, South Carolina*
Hills of Lakeway, *nr Austin, Texas*
Inverness, *Toledo, Ohio*
Medinah, *nr Chicago, Illinios*
Merion, *Ardmore, nr Philadelphia, Pennsylvania*
Muirfield Village, *Dublin, nr Columbus, Ohio*
National Golf Links of America, *Southampton, Long Island, New York*
Oakland Hills, *Birmingham, Michigan*
Oakmont, *Pittsburgh, Pennsylvania*
Oak Tree, *Edmond, Oklahoma*
Olympic, *San Francisco, California*
Pebble Beach, *Pebble Beach, California*
PGA West, *Palm Springs, California*
Pinehurst, *Pinehurst, North Carolina*
Pine Valley, *Clementon, New Jersey*
Princeville, *Kauai, Hawaii*
Riviera, *Pacific Palisades, Los Angeles, California*
Shinnecock Hills, *Southampton, Long Island, New York*
Shoal Creek, *Birmingham, Alabama*
Spanish Bay, *Pebble Beach, California*
Spyglass Hill, *Pebble Beach, California*
Tournament Players Club, *Ponte Vedra, Jacksonville, Florida*
Winged Foot, *Mamaroneck, New York*

West Germany
Hamburger, *Hamburg*

Index of golfers